THE KING'S SON OR A MEMOIR OF BILLY BRAY

# THE KING'S SON

## OR
## A MEMOIR OF BILLY BRAY

COMPILED CHIEFLY FROM HIS OWN MEMORANDA

BY
F.W. BOURNE

## SCRIPTURE TESTIMONY EDITION

WALKING TOGETHER PRESS
ESTES PARK · JENTA MANGORO

Published in 2025 by
Walking Together Press
Estes Park, Colorado USA
Jenta Mangoro, Jos, Plateau Nigeria
walkingtogether.press

Paperback ISBN: 978-1-961568-37-2
eBook ISBN: 978-1-961568-38-9

Cover design by D. Thaine Norris
Typeset in Adobe Garamond Pro by Peter Kurdor

# ABOUT THE SCRIPTURE TESTIMONY EDITION

THIS NARRATIVE invites us to experience the extraordinary life of William "Billy" Bray, an unassuming mine worker whose profound faith and exuberant spirit made him a beacon of Christian devotion, affecting the lives of countless individuals. Born into the harsh realities of 19th-century Cornwall, Billy's journey from a life of utter debauchery to one of unwavering devotion is a testament to the transformative power of faith in Christ Jesus. This memoir paints a portrait of a man whose infectious joy and unshakable belief in God left an indelible mark on all who crossed his path.

Billy's story challenges us to reconsider our own capacity for joy, gratitude, and selfless service. In reintroducing this timeless account to a new generation of readers, we hope to offer not just a historical document, but a wellspring of inspiration—a reminder that God can use any man, even a lowly mine worker and even you.

Data science reveals trends and patterns in information. The *Scripture Testimony Index* is an extensive research project using artificial intelligence and data science to develop a New-Testament-driven subject index across a large body of missionary biographies and personal narratives. As the story enthusiasts at Walking Together Press study these books programmatically; beautiful, bright threads emerge—threads of prayer, provision, deliverance, specific leading, healing, transformation, revival, and miraculous conversion. The end result is an index of thousands of short story excerpts organized by subject and Bible verse that empirically demonstrate the truth of the Scriptures, and which is freely available on our website at walkingtogether.life. Another result of this research was the discovery of dozens of great books that are long out of print and in danger of being forgotten. The *Scripture Testimony Collection* is a set of such books that we enthusiastically recommend, to the degree that we are making the effort to republish them.

Walking Together Press has enhanced this classic title, *The King's Son or A Memoir of Billy Bray*, by identifying and marking twenty-nine portions of the narrative that illustrate specific Biblical topics and verses. An extensive *Scripture Testimony Index* has also been added containing short summaries of how each Scriptural topic is illustrated, making locating specific stories easy. Furthermore, this title is one of many in the *Scripture Testimony Collection*.

# PREFACE TO THE THIRD EDITION

THE RAPID sale of two editions of this Memoir is sufficient evidence of the truth of the remark, that no person in Cornwall, in the humbler ranks of life at least, was better known or more respected than William, commonly called "Billy" Bray. His witty and eccentric sayings caused him to be thus widely known, and his deep and fervent piety to be as generally respected.

It is Billy Bray himself who mostly speaks in the following pages, and while his gems of thought and experience might have been made—by cutting and polishing and more skilful setting—to flash with an intenser light and a purer lustre, I wish to express my gratitude for the numerous testimonies I have received as to the acceptability and usefulness of this little work.

To several ministers whose names occur in the Memoirs, to the Rev. W. Haslam, and to Mr John Ashworth of Rochdale, I tender my heartiest thanks for the interesting incidents which they have kindly furnished.

A grand-daughter of Billy's has a pecuniary interest in the sale of the book, and I hope for her sake, and that, by the blessing of God, it may strengthen the faith, confirm the love, and stimulate the zeal of many, it may obtain a yet wider circulation.

F. W. B.

London, February 5, 1872.

# PREFACE TO THE ELEVENTH EDITION

THIS EDITION is substantially the same as the last, but a few additions have been made, to render the Memoir more complete. For the favour it continues to receive, and for the blessing of God, which still manifestly rests upon it, I wish to express my heartiest thanks.

London, April 12, 1875.

# CONTENTS

# THE KING'S SON

## CHAPTER I.

### HIS CONVERSION.

*"Therefore if any man be in Christ, he is a new creature: old things are passed away; behold, all things are become new."* — *2 Corinthians 5:17.*

HIS chapter, which is mainly devoted to Billy's own account of his conversion, is a striking illustration of this Scripture. Persons who only knew him after this great change had been wrought in his heart by the Truth and the Spirit of God, would never have imagined that he had "run" to that "excess of riot" which he so feelingly describes. But the same grace which transformed a persecuting Saul of Tarsus into the renowned Apostle of the Gentiles, and a blaspheming tinker of Bedford into one of "England's most famous preachers and confessors," changed also Billy Bray, formerly a drunken and lascivious

1

miner, into a loving and consistent disciple of the Son of God, a living embodiment of the things which are "true," and "honest" and "just," and "pure," and "lovely," and of "good report."

The greatness and thoroughness of the change he mercifully experienced fully agree with those representations of it with which all New

| SCRIPTURE TESTIMONY |
| :---: |
| *Salvation transforms* |
| 2 CORINTHIANS 5:16-17 · GALATIANS 6:15 |

Testament readers are so well acquainted. It was a change from darkness to light, from hatred to love, from despair to hope, from misery to joy, from death to life. If the darkness was dense, the light into which his soul was ushered was "marvellous," revealing a new world of spiritual glories and realities; if the hatred was bitter, the subsequent love was self-sacrificing and complete; if the despair was tormenting and terrible, the hope was correspondingly peaceful and bright; if the misery was profound, it was succeeded by "joy that was unspeakable, and full of glory;" and if the death was like the shadow and the actual precursor of the "second death," the life was spiritual and divine, God's own immortal and glorious life in the human soul.

But of the great and gracious change, the reality of which his whole life afterwards testified, Billy Bray shall presently speak himself. It is only necessary for us to state that he was born at Twelveheads, a village in the parish of Kea, near Truro, Cornwall, on the 1st of June 1794. The village then consisted of only a few thatched cottages, inhabited by "tinners," but which had its humble Methodist chapel, where his paternal grandfather worshipped, and which he had helped to build. He was one of the old Methodists, for he joined the then persecuted and despised people when Mr Wesley first visited Cornwall. Billy's father was also pious, but he died when his children were very young, who then went to live with their grandfather; and with him Billy remained until he was seventeen years old, when he went to Devonshire, where, far removed from pious example and instruction, he "lived a bad life." He says:

"I became the companion of drunkards, and during that time I was very near hell. I remember once getting drunk in Tavistock; when going home we met a large horse in the way; it was late at night, and two of us got on the horse's back; we had not gone far before the horse stumbled against a stone, and, turning right over, both of us were nearly killed. At another time I got drunk, and while fighting with a man my hat fell into the fire, and was burnt. I stole another to wear home, and narrowly escaped being sent to jail for it."

His drunken frolics were many, which he could not recall without deep shame and sorrow; but his soul was stained with viler sins than any that have been mentioned. His gratitude was lively ever afterwards because the Lord had saved him "from the lowest hell." "The Lord was good to me," he often said, "when I was the servant of the devil, oh I should have been down in hell now;" and he felt he must praise the Lord for His goodness. His hairbreadth escapes from danger, though he was such a wicked wretch, made an impression on his heart at the time, and a deeper impression afterwards. He was emphatic in his wish that all the evil should be faithfully recorded, that the great mercy of God might be more fully known. "Once," he tells us, "I was working underground, and I heard a 'scat'(rent) overhead; I ran out, and, I think, forty tons fell down where I had been working but a minute before."

But he had not yet reached the lowest depths of evil and misery. Turned away from the mine at which he worked for being insolent to the "captain," he removed to another part of Devonshire, and as if to make his damnation sure, went to live at a beer-shop. We may follow the course of his narrative again:

"There, with other drunkards, I drank all night long. But I had a sore head and a sick stomach, and worse than all, horrors of mind that no tongue can tell. I used to dread to go to sleep for fear of waking up in hell; and though I made many promises to the Lord to be better, I was soon as bad or worse than ever. After being absent from my native county seven years, I returned a *drunkard*"

A whole world of misery that one word expresses and reveals. Domestic happiness can find no place in the home of a drunkard. His infatuation is as complete as it is terrible. The wife of a drunkard, the child of a drunkard, how much they stand in need of help and pity is only known to God. Billy well knew that the wife of a drunkard has reason to praise

God when her husband is saved from intemperance if nobody else has. His wife, he tells us, had to fetch him home night after night from the beer-shop.

| SCRIPTURE TESTIMONY |
| --- |
| *Whatever you ask in prayer, in* *faith, abiding, you will receive* |
| MATTHEW 21:22 · MARK 11:24 · JOHN 15:7 · I JOHN 5:14-15 |

"At one time I remember I went to get some coal; there was a beer-shop in the way" [alas! that there are so many beer-shops, for every one of them is *in the way* of some poor drunkard], "and coming home I went in, and stayed till I got drunk. My poor wife was forced to come for me, and wheel home the coal herself. A drunkard would rather spend his money in drink than give it to his wife and children. At one time I had good wages for two months successively, and £5 of the money went in drink. I sinned against light and knowledge; and never got drunk without being condemned for it;" his conscience tormented him by day, and dreams terrified him by night.

But the crisis of his life was now at hand. He was about to be recovered to truth and holiness, and Bunyan's "Visions of Heaven and Hell" was the appointed means of his recovery. The book came into his hands, and he began to read it, the "Visions of Heaven" first, and then the "Visions of Hell." Bunyan saw, he says, two lost souls in hell cursing each other, for being the author of each other's misery, and that they who love one another on earth will hate one another in hell. One of Billy's companions, to whom he was much attached, was also much attached to him. They worked together, and went to the alehouse and got drunk together. The arrow that pierced his soul was the thought, "Shall S. Coad and I, who like each other so much, *torment* each other in hell?"

From that time, November 1823, he had a strong desire to be a better man. He had married some time before; his wife had been converted when young, but had gone back from the right way before marriage. The remembrance of what she had enjoyed was very sweet, and yet very bitter. She told her husband that "no tongue could tell what they enjoy who serve the Lord." "Why don't you begin again?" was his pertinent inquiry; adding, "for then I may begin too." He was ashamed to fall on his knees before his wife, "for the devil had such a hold of him;" but he knew it was his duty to pray for mercy. He went to bed without bending his knees in prayer; but about three o'clock he awoke, and thinking that if he waited until his wife was converted that he might never be saved ("though he had begged she would get converted first, and then show him how to be saved, for he thought she was so much less a sinner than himself that she would soon be forgiven"), he jumped out of bed *and got on his knees for the first time*, and forty years afterwards he could joyfully boast that he had never once since been ashamed to pray. His decision, once formed, was unalterable, "and I found," he said, "that the more I prayed the more I felt to pray." The whole forenoon was spent in supplication. If he had been less I resolute and in earnest, the day of grace might have passed unimproved, the blessed opportunity have fled for ever. Forty years ago, on pay-days and setting-days,[1] miners in Cornwall were in the habit of going to the alehouse to eat, drink, and get drunk. This day, so auspiciously begun, was one of those days, and Billy joined his companions as usual. "I was the worst of the lot," is his own expression. "He was the wildest, most daring and reckless of all the reckless, daring men; and on one occasion so fearful was his blasphemy, that his wicked comrades declared *that his oaths must come from hell, for they smelt of sulphur.* "His liveliness of disposition, his power of repartee, his mother-wit marked him out from others, and the same remarkable natural powers were used to produce merriment and laughter, and to turn sacred subjects into ridicule and fun, that subsequently made him so popular and useful as a follower of the Saviour and a preacher of His gospel. The change in him was noticed by his companions, and one of them swore. This elicited the reproof, "You must give an account of that some day," when the other mockingly answered, "Shall we all go to the 'Bryanites'[2] meeting?" to which Billy replied it was better to go there than to hell. Reproached by another "for making such a noise, he replied, 'You would roar out too, if you felt my load, and roar I will until I get it off.'"

On the first pay-day that he came home sober for many years, his wife, he says, "was greatly surprised and asked, 'How is it you are come home

---

1  Days appointed for making contracts for work.
2  So the Bible Christians were then generally called

so early to-night?' and she had for answer, 'You will never see me drunk again, by the help of the Lord.' And she never has since. Praise the Lord He can cure drunkards.

"That same night I went up-stairs, and prayed till we went to bed. The next day I did not go to work; I took the Bible and Wesley's Hymn-Book, went up-stairs, and read and prayed all day. Sometimes I read the Bible, sometimes the Hymn-Book, and then I cried to the Lord for mercy. I was glad that I had begun to seek the Lord, for it is said, 'Let the heart of him rejoice that seeketh the Lord.' When Sunday morning came it was very wet; the 'Bible Christians' had a class-meeting a mile from our house; I went to the place, but because it was, wet none, came."

This had an unfavourable effect on his mind, and his first thought was, "If a little rain will keep the people away from the house of God, I shall not join here." This hasty decision was soon reversed, for Billy was a consistent member with the Bible Christians for more than forty years, and died in communion with the people of his early choice. But how much harm lukewarm and careless professors do to inquirers after salvation and young converts it is impossible to determine. The class-meeting has perhaps been a greater benefit to Methodism than any of her institutions besides. To multitudes it has been a safeguard in danger, a comfort in trouble. But in these, in some respects, degenerate days, attendance at the class-meeting is by many deemed unnecessary and in some quarters it has become quite unfashionable.

The results are such as might have been predicted with certainty. The example of the older members is most disastrous in its effects on the habits of the younger ones, and a feeble, stunted piety is, unhappily, characteristic of too many of our churches.

But Billy returned home, and alone with God, with the Bible and the Hymn-Book as his companions, he spent all that day in reading and praying. He was assailed fiercely by the temptation "that he would never find mercy;" but with the promise, "Seek, and ye shall find," he quenched this fiery dart of the wicked one, and in due time he learnt, by blessed experience, that the promise was *true*. Monday forenoon was spent in the same manner. In the afternoon he had to go to the mine, but "all the while I was working I was crying to the Lord for mercy." His sad state moved his fellow-workmen to pity; he "was not like Billy Bray," they said. Why? Because he formerly told lies to make them laugh, and now he was determined to serve the Lord. No relief came, and he went home, "asking for mercy all the way." It was then eleven o'clock at night, but the first thing he did was to go up-stairs and fall upon his knees, and entreat God to have mercy on him. Everything else was forgotten in the intensity of his desire that the Lord would speak peace to his soul. After a while he went to bed, but not to sleep. All the forenoon of the next day he spent in crying for mercy, food being almost untasted, and conversation with his "partner" at the mine in the afternoon nearly ceased. That day passed away, and nearly the whole night he spent upon his knees. The enemy "thrust at him sore," but "I was glad," he says, "that I had begun to seek the Lord, for I felt *I would rather be crying for mercy than living in sin.*" On the next day he had "almost laid hold of the blessing," but the time came for him to go to the mine (two o'clock in the afternoon). The devil strongly tempted him while at his work that he would never find mercy; "but I said to him, 'Thou art a liar, devil,' and as soon as I said so, I felt the weight gone from my mind, and I could praise the Lord, but not with that liberty I could afterwards. So I called to my comrades, 'I am not so happy as some, but sooner than I would go back to sin again, I would be put in that "plat"¹ there, and burned to death.'" When he got home on former nights he had not cared anything about supper, his anguish of soul being so great, nor did he this night, because a hope had sprung up in his heart, and with it a determination to press right into the kingdom of heaven. To his chamber he again repaired. Beautifully simple and touching are his own, words. "I said to the Lord, 'Thou hast said, *They that ask shall receive, they that seek shall find, and to them that knock the door shall be opened,* and I have faith to believe it.' In an instant the Lord made me so happy that I cannot express what I felt. I shouted for joy. I praised God with my whole heart for what He had done for a poor sinner like me; for I could say, The Lord hath pardoned all my sins. I think this was in November 1823, but what day of the month I do not know. I remember this, that everything

---

1   An open space near the shaft of a mine.

looked new to me, the people, the fields, the cattle, the trees. I was like a man in a new world. I spent the greater part of my time in praising the Lord. I could say with Isaiah, 'O Lord, I will praise Thee, for though Thou wast angry with me, Thine anger is turned away, and Thou comfortedst me;' or like David, 'The Lord hath brought me up out of a horrible pit of mire and clay, and set my feet upon a rock, and established my goings, and *hath put a new song* in my mouth, even praise unto my God.' I was a new man altogether. I told all I met what the Lord had done for my soul. I have heard some say that they have had hard work to get away from their companions, but I sought mine out, and had hard work to find them soon enough to tell them what the Lord had done for me. Some said I was mad; and others that they should get me back again next pay-day. But, praise the Lord, it is now more than forty years ago, and they have not got me yet. They said I was a *mad-man*, but they meant I was a *glad-man*, and, glory be to God! I have been glad ever since."

# CHAPTER II.

## THE FIRST-FRUITS OF HARVEST

*"Of His own will begat He us with the word of truth, that we should be a kind of first-fruits of His creatures"* — *James 1:18.*

BILLY BRAY's own account of his conversion bears the impress of truth and reality. The sceptic who tried to reason him out of his convictions, or to rob him of his perfect peace, his living joy, his immortal hope, utterly failed. I have witnessed some such attempts; but, as Billy said, they had no more effect than "a drop of water upon a duck's back." If nothing is so divine as experience, and if the deeper it is the diviner, Billy had good reason to be satisfied with his. His was no ordinary struggle, but it ended in perfect liberty of soul. He could say—

> *"No* condemnation now I dread."

The conflict was terrible, but the victory was all the more glorious. The trial of his faith was sharp, but the reward was sweeter ever afterwards. He knew more certainly, how inconceivably great and glorious was the salvation which is by faith in Christ Jesus with eternal glory. He was filled with a holy rapture of soul, which nothing could restrain. His words, his tones, his looks, had a magnetic power. He was, so to speak, charged with a divine electricity, and the effects thereof were sudden and marvellous. He could no more help speaking of Christ and His salvation than the sun can help shining, or

*Hicks' Mill Chapel.*

the trees in spring can help budding and blossoming into beauty and life.
The light that was kindled flashed with unusual splendour, but it increased
in brightness even unto the end. His wife was the first to yield to his holy
entreaties, and about a week afterwards in Hicks' Mill Chapel (which has
been, happily, the birthplace of hundreds of souls) she regained the blessing
she had lost. He had spent much of his time in his unconverted state in
telling lies to "make fun," as his companions called it; "but now I could tell
them a new tale about heavenly truths, and what the Lord had done for
me." This was not so pleasing to many; but "it was not long before some of
them were as mad as I was." The open confession of Christ is a solemn duty
of His followers; it is an inestimable privilege also. How much this duty is
neglected, how much this privilege is despised, multitudes know to their
sorrow. Billy's words thrill us with joy, and yet produce much self-reproach
and self-condemnation as we transcribe them.

"There were men who professed to be converted before I was, but did not
love the Lord enough to own Him, and us enough to pray with us and tell
us we were going to hell. But when I was converted, praise the Lord, He gave
me strength to tell all I met with, that I was happy, and that what the Lord
had done for me He would do for anybody else that would seek His face.

There was nobody that prayed in the mine where I worked; but when the Lord converted my soul He gave me power to pray with the men before we went to our different places to work. Sometimes I felt it a heavy cross, but the cross is the way to the crown. Sometimes I have had as many as from six to ten men down with me, and I have said, 'Now, if you will hearken to me, I will pray for you before we go to work, for if I did not pray with you, and any of us should be killed, I should think it was my fault.' Some of them would say, 'You pray and we will hear you.' Then I should pray in what people call simple language, but as I hope the Lord would have me. When praying I used to say, 'Lord, if any of us must be killed, or die to-day, let it be *me;* let not one of these men die, for they are not happy ; but I am, and if I die to-day I shall go to heaven.' When I rose from my knees, I should see the tears running down their faces; and soon after some of them became praying men too."

The individual cases of conversion are too numerous for us to relate here; but one or two may be given as specimens of the rest.

"An old man, called William S----, with his son, used to work near me, and as they were not converted I used to tell them what the Lord was willing to do for them, and then I would kneel down and pray for them until the tears came into the old man's eyes. But such power has the devil over poor sinners, that soon after I should hear him swearing at his son. And I was tempted not to pray with him again, but, thank the Lord, I did not yield to the temptation. I continued to pray with him, and before the poor old man died he was made very happy in Jesus."

O Christian reader! "of some have compassion, making a difference: and others save with fear, *pulling them out of the fire!* "If every convert only felt that he was a *voice for Christ,* how many would hear the gospel that go down into the grave in silence; if every one only felt that he was a *hand for Christ,* how many would be snatched from death and destruction who now become an easy prey to the Evil One. Take another case:

"There was Justin T----, who was with me in Devonshire; we were companions in drunkenness, and came home to Cornwall at the same time. I was converted before he was;

| SCRIPTURE TESTIMONY |
| --- |
| *The sheep know and hear His voice* |
| JOHN 10:3-4 · JOHN 10:16 |

and when I told my comrades what danger the wicked were in, and where they would go if they died in sin, they would persecute me, and call me a fool. But J. T. used to say, 'You shall leave that man alone, and say nothing to him, for I knew him when he was a drunkard, and now he is a good man; I wish I was like him.' *Then my heart went out after J. T.* One day when at work in the field, I knelt down to pray for him. *The Lord spoke to my mind, 'I will save him soon.'* When I next saw him I told him I had good news for him, for while I was out in the field praying for him the Lord told me he should be converted soon. *And so he was.* Shortly after his conversion he was taken ill. I saw him many times in his illness, and he told me he was happy in Jesus, and going to heaven to praise God for ever."

Some parts of this narrative may appear to be strange and inexplicable even to some of the Lord's children. They never heard the Lord speak to them in the way just described. Would that they had! For when God impresses persons to pray for any particular blessing, it is, a sure sign that He is about to bestow that blessing upon them. Definiteness of aim in prayer, combined with a holy persistency, will surely hit the mark. We quote just one more case, as it illustrates Billy's quickness of thought, and the happy way in which he could turn a phrase, for which he was so remarkable.

SCRIPTURE TESTIMONY

*There is no sting in death for the believer*

I CORINTHIANS 15:54-57

"I worked with a man before I was converted called *William Bray*, and he was, like myself, a very wicked man. Both of us were promoted at the same time, for he was made 'captain' of the mine, and I was adopted into the royal family of heaven, and made a child of God. I had not seen him for a long time, when one Monday evening it was impressed on my mind that if I went to see him he would be saved. And I went, nothing doubting, and found him at home I prayed with him; told him what the Lord would do for him; and soon he found the Saviour, and was made happy in His love. I saw him many times in his last sickness, and he was very happy and full of faith. Just before he died he sent for me, as he wanted to tell me that Christ was his. Then he had a good shout, and said, 'Christ is mine, and I am His.' These were the last words he spoke to me, and soon after he was taken to paradise. Since then, four of his children have gone to meet him, and his wife will no doubt soon, for she too is in the road to heaven."

Mr Ashworth truly says that Billy was one of those happy, unselfish men who love everybody, and with simple earnestness he spoke to all—rich or poor—about the love of Jesus. He gloried in religious revivals, and shouted for joy when he heard of souls being saved anywhere."

Mr A. illustrates this trait of his character by relating an extraordinary incident, full details of which the Rev. W. Haslam, of Little Missenden, Bucks, has, at my request, kindly supplied. He says: —

"I had often heard of Billy Bray at Baldhu, from his brother James, and wished very much to see him. One morning, three months after my conversion,[1] I heard some one walking about in the hall of my house,

---

1  The reader will be interested in the following account of the conversion of this good clergyman, from his own pen. "In the hey-day of my prosperity, and in the success of my sacramental ministrations, while I thought the church was the Ark—and no salvation could be had out of the church, except by some uncovenanted mercy—one of my most promising disciples, a regular communicant and zealous churchman, was taken seriously ill, and was pronounced to be in hopeless 'galloping consumption.' The man was my own servant, a gardener, and one to whom I was much attached; not exactly my spiritual child in the gospel, but my ecclesiastical child in churchmanship, and a strong adherent who, with many others, upheld me and encouraged me in a place abounding with 'gospel men,' against Dissenters of various kinds. This man's heart failed him in the prospect of death; his views and religious practices did not comfort him in the hour of need, or give him assurance. He heard of others who could say their sins were pardoned, and read their title clear to mansions in the skies, whereas, with his, as he thought, superior teaching, he was yet afraid to die. He ventured to send for some Dissenter to talk to him and pray with him, who went to work in a way just the reverse of the priest. Instead of building up and comforting, the man plainly showed him he was a lost sinner, and needed to come to Jesus, just as he was, for salvation and pardon. The man was confident, 'Pray for yourself,' said he; and he set before him the finished work of Christ, as the sinner's substitute. The gardener was brought under deep conviction, and eventually found pardon and peace through the blood of Jesus. This was a great disappointment. Instead of rejoicing with Christ over a lost sheep which he had found, I was angry with the sheep for being found, and deeply mourned over what I considered a fall into schism! Grieved as I was, however, I loved my disciple, and went to see him, though not till after several urgent invitations to go. I endeavoured to reclaim him, but the man was too firmly persuaded to be shaken from 'the truth as it is in Jesus.' Instead of lying on a bed of suffering, he was walking about the room, praising God in a most joyful state. 'Ah, John, you are excited, you have been taking wine!' 'No, master,' said the man, 'I have not touched a drop of it—no, dear no, that is not it, dear master. I know you love me and I love you—you don't know this joy and peace, I am sure you don't, or you would have told me of it. O master I pray the Lord to give it to you—I will never rest praying for you—don't be angry with me—the Lord bless you and

'praising the Lord.' I rose from the breakfast table, and opened the door to see who my happy, unceremonious visitor could be; —and then for the first time beheld this queer looking man. I asked him who he was. He replied, with a face beaming with joy—

"'I am Billy Bray—be you the "passon?"'

"'Yes,' I answered.

"'Converted, are ye?'

"'Yes, thank God.'

"'Be the missus converted?'

"'Yes.'

"'Thank the dear Lord,' said he, coming into the room to make his bow to the said missus. Then he inquired of her if she had any maids in the house.

"'Yes, there are three.'

"'Are they converted?'

"'Yes.'

"'Where be they?'

"'In the kitchen.' So he proceeded thither, and soon we heard them all praising the Lord in Cornish style with a loud voice.

"After a time Billy joined us again in the dining-room, to take, by invitation, some breakfast, but before he sat down he approached me and suddenly put his arm round me, and took me up, and carried me round the table, and then, setting me down at my chair, rolled on the floor for

---

convert your soul! You have been a kind good friend to me, I cannot forget or leave you. I will pray for you while I live, for the Lord to save your soul.' I could not stand this pleading, and fled from the house in a tumult of disappointment and confusion." His heart was now "broken for work." A visit to a brother clergyman deepened his convictions; for he plainly told him that "if he had been converted he would have rejoiced in that man's salvation and praised God with him, and that he would never do any good in his parish till he was converted himself," "So deep became his distress, that, when the bell tolled for service on the following Sunday morning, he trembled and feared to preach;" but while preaching on the words—*What think ye of Christ?* the Lord showed him so clearly that Christ was the true and only foundation, the Lamb of God that taketh away the sin of the world, that his soul was filled with joy, "as full of joy as it had been of misery!" The fervour and earnestness with which he now proclaimed "a present salvation caused a general cry for mercy, and many of his parishioners were saved." It was no wonder that Billy wished to see him, to *give his eyes a treat,* and to witness some of the blessed results of his prayer of faith years before.

joy, and said he was as 'happy as he could live.'[1] We persuaded him to sit down and get some breakfast, as he had been riding in a slow-going donkey cart since midnight through the cold night air of January. He said he had heard of our conversion, and had been begging Father to give him leave to visit us. He received permission to do so just as he was getting into bed at half-past eleven. So he put up his clothes again, and 'hitched in the donkey,' and came along singing all the way.

"Then he proceeded to tell us why he was so anxious to see us. He said, some years before that time he was walking over the place where the house stands, and the Lord said to him, 'I will give thee all that dwell on this mountain.' So he knelt down immediately and prayed for all who lived there, and then proceeded to the various cottages which were situated on that hill, and continued to visit the people in those cottages till they were all brought to the Lord. Then he knelt down and complained that there were 'only three housen' there, and received a promise that there should be some more. He never forgot this, but continually mentioned it in his prayers to the Lord till, to his joy, one day he received a letter from his brother James to say they were planting the hill and going to build a church there, and then his brother wrote to say they were building a house (the Vicarage)—then again another house (the School). Dear Billy redoubled his efforts of prayer and faith, and when the church was opened he came to see and hear for himself, and was disgusted and disappointed to find a 'Pusey there preaching.' He went away unhappy, and it came to his mind that he had no business to come to see till Father had bidden. So he departed to the neighbourhood of Bodmin where he then lived, and remained there. After a few years news reached him of the clergyman's

---

1 Many persons have been treated by Billy in much the same way as the good clergyman. The first time Mr Maynard saw him was at Deliverance Chapel in 1844 under these circumstances. When he was in the pulpit a little man came in, turning up the white of his eyes, and praising the Lord. He thought at once, as the eyes of all the people were instantly upon the new-comer, and as a smile, as if a magic-wand had been used, passed over their faces, "This, then, is the famous Billy Bray, about whom I have heard so much" After the service, Billy did not exactly carry the preacher, but he dragged him round the pulpit pew to the amusement of the people, shouting and jumping with all his might the whole time. When he let the preacher go, he asked him whether he could stand that or not. "Yes, much more than that," was the answer. "All right, friend Maynard, praise the Lord."

*Baldhu Vicarage.*

conversion, and also that there was a great revival in the place. He then
praised God and begged permission to go and see this passon and his
missus, and continued to beg till he obtained permission.[1]

"After breakfast he went off to the school-house, and found the school-
master and his wife both converted, then to another house where the
people were all converted. His joy was unbounded, he jumped and danced,
and clapped his hands, he shouted and he sang! The happy man was beside
himself, and beyond himself."

He began to publicly exhort men to repent, and turn to God, about
a year after his conversion. Towards the end of 1824 his name was put
on the Local Preachers' Plan, and his labours were much blessed in the
conversion of souls. He did not commonly select a text, as is the general
habit of preachers, but he usually began his addresses by reciting a verse
of a hymn, a little of his own experience, or some telling anecdote. But he
had the happy art of pleasing and profiting the people, so that persons of
all ages, the young as much as the old, of all classes, the rich as much as

1   On my first interview with him he carried me round the room many times, continually asking me, "Is not this 'pretty' riding, dear?" But I was too much disconcerted,
half-amused, half-frightened, to be able to answer.

the poor, and of all characters, the worldly as much as the pious, flocked to hear him, and he retained his popularity until the last. As the Rev. M. G. Pearse says, "From one end of Cornwall to another no name is more familiar than that of Billy Bray.

"On Sundays, when one met crowds of strangers making for the little white-washed chapel that was perched up amongst the granite boulders, or when one found the quiet 'church town ' thronged by the well-dressed people, the usual explanation was that Billy Bray was going to preach.

"If you had overtaken Billy on the way you could not have been long in doubt as to who he was. A little, spare, wiry man, whose dress of orthodox black, and the white tie, indicated the preacher. The sharp, quick, discerning eye that looked out from under the brows, the mouth almost hard in its decision, all the face softened by the light that played constantly upon it, and by the happy wrinkles round the eyes, and the smile that had perpetuated itself, —these belonged to no ordinary man. And with the first suspicion that this was Billy Bray there would quickly come enough to confirm it. If you gave him half a chance there would certainly be a straightforward question about your soul, in wise, pithy words. And if the answer was what it should be, the lanes would ring with his happy thanksgiving."

I remember once hearing him speak with great effect to a large congregation, principally miners. In that neighbourhood there were two mines, one very prosperous, and the other quite the reverse, for the work was hard, and the wages low. He represented himself as working at *that* mine, but on the "pay-day" going to the prosperous one for his wages. But had he not been at work at the other mine? the manager inquired. He had, but he liked the wages at the good mine the best. He pleaded very earnestly, but in vain. He was dismissed at last with the remark, from which there was no appeal, that he must come there to work if he came there for his wages. And then he turned upon the congregation, and the effect was almost irresistible, that they must serve Christ here if they would share His glory hereafter, but if they would serve the devil now, to him they must go for their wages by and by.

If he quoted the wonderful saying of our Lord, "I am the bread of life," he would proceed in some such strain as this: "Precious loaf this! The patriarchs and prophets eat of this loaf, and never found a bit of crust about it. The apostles and martyrs eat of this loaf, too, for many long years and never found a bit of ' vinny' in it. And, bless the Lord! poor old Billy Bray can eat it without teeth, and get fat on it."

Mr Tabb says that at the opening of Trecrogo Chapel, in the Launceston Circuit, the crowd that came to hear Billy was so great they were obliged to have the service in a field. The subject of his address was "Happiness," and, as his custom was, he interspersed his discourse with some pointed remarks on Teetotalism. Thinking that some of his hearers would probably think he was pressing the duty of self-denial and self-sacrifice too closely, he burst out—"*You* may think *we* have nothing to drink, but we have. My father keeps a wine-shop." An apt reference to Isaiah 25:6 followed. And his imagination once fired, the most fastidious could listen to him with pleasure, and even the wise and learned to edification. At such times he would generally express his determination to live up to his glorious priv-ileges, and enjoy the varied *abundance* of his Father's house. Some could only eat out of the *silent* dish, but he could eat out of that, and out of the *shouting* dish, and *jumping* dish, and every other.

His *preaching* was effectual because he prayed much. By prayer he opened God's hand when it was filled with blessings, and by prayer,

| SCRIPTURE TESTIMONY |
| --- |
| *The believer is to be persistent in prayer* |
| LUKE 11:5-10 |

too, he kept the devil under restraint, who was to Billy Bray, as we shall clearly see further on, just as he was to Martin Luther, and John Bunyan, and George Fox, a very real person. This is strikingly characteristic of him. Mr Maynard says, "Many a time, when he and I have been leaving my home together, he has said to me, ' Now, friend Maynard, let us pray a minute before we go, or else the devil will be scratching me on the way. If I leave without praying, this is the way he serves me; but when I get on my knees a minute or two before leaving I cut his ould(old) claws, and then he can't harm me: so I always like to cut his claws before I go.'"

There was great excitement, and much apparent confusion, in some of his meetings, more than sufficient to shock the prejudices of high-ly-sensitive and refined, or over-fastidious persons. Billy could not tolerate "deadness," as he expressively called it, either in a professing Christian or in a meeting. He had a deeper sympathy with persons singing, or shouting, or leaping for joy than he had with

> "The speechless awe that dares not move,
> And all the silent heaven of love;"

but his services, with all their simplicity and warmth, were distasteful only to a few, and many were so far convinced that his method was right, or were so far influenced and attracted, as heartily to join with him. He speaks of one who worked with him in Devonshire, and returned at the same time to Cornwall. They were also converted together, but while Billy joined the Bible Christians, his companion cast in his lot with the Wesleyan Methodists. Their names were put on the plan at the same time, and when Billy was appointed at a chapel near where his friend lived he came to hear him, but would leave immediately after the preacher had done speaking, as he could not enjoy the subsequent proceedings, some singing, some praying, some shouting, some dancing, scenes to be frequently witnessed when the Cornish people get what they call the "victory" through the blood of the Lamb. But one Saturday night John had a dream which brought him to the conclusion that he was wrong in opposing shouting when the Lord made His people happy. The next night, and ever afterwards, he remained until the end, and "shouted" as loudly and "leaped" as joyfully as Billy himself. He lived a good life, and died a happy death; Billy dismissing him with the characteristic remark—"So he has done with the *doubters*, and is got up with the *shouters*."

# CHAPTER III.

## JOY UNSPEAKABLE AND FULL OF GLORY.

*"Whom having not seen, ye love; in whom, though now ye see Him not, yet believing, ye rejoice with joy unspeakable and full of glory." — 1 Peter 1:8.*

*"Rejoice in the Lord alway; and again I say, Rejoice." — Philippians 4:4.*

HENRY WARD Beecher says, "It is always infelicitous when men fall into the habit of speaking of religion as the mother of trials, and of their Christian experience from the side of its restrictions and limitations. . . . When people want to make things attractive in farming, they give exhibitions of their products. The women bring their very best butter, moulded into tempting golden lumps; and the men bring the noblest beets and vegetables of every kind; and from the orchards they bring the rarest fruits, and when you go into the room where all these things are displayed, they seem to you attractive and beautiful. "It seems to me that this is the way a Christian church ought to represent the Christian life. You ought to pile up your apples and pears and peaches and flowers and vegetables, to show what is the positive fruit of religion. But many people in Christian life do as farmers would do who should go to a show, and carry—one, pigweed; another, thistles; another, dock; and another, old hard lumps of clay; and should arrange these worthless things along the sides of the room, and mourn over them. What sort of husbandry would that be? Christians are too apt

21

to represent the dark side of religion in their conversation and meetings."

It was Billy Bray's excellence and glory that he always represented the *bright* side of religion to his fellows; to him, indeed, it had no other. He had a nature that tended "to produce joy;" but whatever may be the temperament of persons, unquestionably "the effect of the whole of religious living is to produce joyfulness."

Payson said on his dying bed, "If men only knew the honour and glory that awaited them in Christ, they would go about the streets crying out, 'I am a Christian! I am a Christian!' that men might rejoice with them in the blessedness of which they were soon to partake." Billy did this all his life long, and verily he had his reward. He tells us, soon after his conversion, "I was very happy in my *work*, and could leap and dance for joy under ground[1] as well as on the surface. My comrades used to tell me, that was no religion, dancing, shouting, and making so much to-do.' But I was born in the *fire*, and could not live in the *smoke*. They said there was no need to leap, and dance, and make so much noise, for the Lord was not deaf, and He knows our hearts. And I would reply, 'But you must know that the devil is not deaf either, and yet his servants make a great noise. The devil would rather see us doubting than hear us shouting.'"

The reader can easily imagine what were Billy's favourite portions of Scripture and hymns, but we may quote one or two of the former that he repeated thousands of times. "Thou hast turned for me my mourning into dancing; Thou hast put off my sackcloth, and girded me with gladness; to the end that my glory may sing praise to Thee, and not be silent. O Lord my God, I will give thanks unto Thee for ever" (Psalm 30:11, 12). "Then shall the virgin rejoice in the dance, both young men and old together, for I will turn their mourning into joy, and will comfort them, and make them rejoice from their sorrow" (Jeremiah 31:13). The idea that these and similar passages had a figurative and not a literal meaning, he held in the greatest contempt. If persons attempted, either playfully or in earnest, to argue the point with him, he would turn upon them all his powers of wit and sarcasm, and all his treasures of experience and Scripture, and such

---

1    Once he said he had felt "the joys of religion at 250!" i.e., "two hundred and fifty fathoms below 'grass.'"

was his holy ardour and impetuosity that from such assaults many found the only safe refuge to be either silence or flight. "David danced," he never forgot to tell us, "before the Lord with all his might;" and that he "and all the house of Israel brought up the ark of the Lord with shouting, and with the sound of a trumpet," and that what David did surely all the people might do under a *happier* dispensation, and that the opposition of the unconverted or formal professors was like that of "Michal, Saul's daughter," who, when she saw "King David leaping and dancing before the Lord," "despised him in her heart." The song of Moses and the children of Israel after they had safely passed through the Red Sea, he also used with excellent effect. To any person who objected to the meetings on account of their noise and uproar, and many have objected to them on that account, he thought it quite enough to say that when the foundation of the second temple was laid "all the people shouted with a great shout," and "that the people could not discern the voice of the shout of joy from the noise of the weeping of the people: for the people shouted with a loud shout, and the noise was heard afar off." On any who said—

> "But what confusion is this here?
> What noise of tumult do I hear?
> How ill it suits this place!"

and who demanded that "calm serenity should prevail" when they worshipped God, that their "pleas," like "tranquil sonnets," might "*gently* pierce the peaceful skies," he would retort "that we must have a *full* joy ourselves to know what a full joy means;" and he hardly ever failed to add, "Our blessed Lord has said, 'Ask, and ye shall receive, *that your joy may be full.*'"

The account of Christ's triumphant entry into Jerusalem was another choice incident, sweeter to his taste than honey or the honeycomb. He used to positively revel in the statements, "And a very great multitude spread their garments in the way; others cut down branches from the trees, and strewed them in the way. And the multitudes that went before, and that followed, cried, saying, Hosanna to the Son of David! Blessed is He that cometh in the name of the Lord! Hosanna in the highest!" And if it happened at the time of a contested election he would sometimes ask, "May all the people shout '-------------- forever!' and no person find fault, and may not Billy Bray shout 'Jesus for ever?'"

Usually, I suppose, his remarks would be to the following effect, as Mr Maynard says that he has so heard him speak many a time: "If this is worth shouting for, our election is worth far more, for those who get elected, and sent up to the House of Commons may soon die, or lose their seat at the next election, consequently their honour and happiness may not last long; but, if we get elected into the Lord's Parliament, and once get into the Parliament House of Heaven, we shall never die, never get turned out; hence, we have more reason to shout than they."

But the narrative of the lame man, "whom they laid daily at the gate of the temple which was called Beautiful," was perhaps most precious of all. "And he leaping up stood, and walked, and entered with them into the temple, walking, and leaping, and praising God." If he made this incident the subject of an address, he would ask if the dear Lord could not now do as He had done in days of old? He had healed a cripple forty years old, who leaped for joy when he was healed; and Billy would "leap," or "run," if he had the chance, and praise God, for had not he as good a right to do so now as that cripple had then—he that was never a cripple and never was lame? —or that he had got something more than lame legs cured, his never-dying soul saved? He ought, he thought, to *leap four feet to his two.* "It was Peter who took the lame man by the hand; but it was the Lord who gave him strength in his ankle-bones, that made him run and leap. He did not praise Peter, he praised the dear Lord; and so would I. It is before the Lord we should leap and dance and shout. Satan has his *merry-men*[1] and they do more wickedness by their actions than by what they say, for actions speak louder than words. Now I am a *merry-man* for the Lord Jesus Christ. He is the best Master, and gives the best wages. The devil gives sorrow for joy; but the Lord gives joy instead of sorrow, 'beauty for ashes, the oil of joy for mourning, and the garment of *praise* for the spirit of heaviness.'"

And is all this to be denounced by men of the world, or by Christians of different temperament, as "foolish extravagance?" Was it not predicted

---

1   A buffoon, a merryandrew.

that "the lame man should leap as a hart, and the tongue of the dumb sing?" Billy could not understand how any could be *dumb* who were "born of the Spirit." They needed at least to pray, "Open Thou my lips, and my mouth shall show forth Thy praise." It seemed natural, at any rate, for him to sing and shout, to leap and dance, and, if we may use the word, to *caper* for joy, for he seemed as free from care, as frolicsome, as gay, as gladsome, as a young lamb dancing in the meadow, or goat upon the mountain crag. His joy was always fresh and pure, exultant and full, even to overflowing. "It is a poor spectacle," he would say, "when we have nothing but the *telling* part of the love of Christ; it is the *feeling* part that makes us happy." His choice friends were neither ashamed to praise the Lord in the *market* nor in the *great congregation*. Many a long journey, either alone or with such companions—"birds of a feather," was his expression—has he taken, and praised the Lord all the way. He could say with the poet—

> "Winter nights and summer days
> Are far too short to sing His praise."

I remember taking a walk with him early one morning, when his conversation was of heaven. He stopped, as if a thought had suddenly occurred to him. He remained silent

SCRIPTURE TESTIMONY

*Disciples were filled with joy and the Holy Spirit*

ACTS 13:52

for a moment with uplifted eyes, which almost immediately filled with tears; a "Praise the Lord!" escaped his lips, and he bounded away, though an old man, like a hart or deer. When I came up to him he was praising the Lord aloud, as if it was the business of his life, and said, "My dear brother, if I only lived to my privilege, I should not feel the ground over which I walk."

At a district meeting held at Hicks Mill, in 1866, Mr Oliver in describing the triumphant death of a woman, said she died shouting Victory. This touched Billy's heart, and he shouted "Glory! If a *dying* woman praised the Lord, I should think a living man might."

He would commonly address his fellow-Christians thus! "You praise God, and I will praise God, and we will both praise God together;" or,

"You be the parson, and I'll be the clerk; —you say, 'Praise the Lord,' and I'll say, 'Amen!' or I'll be the parson, and you shall be the clerk—I'll say, 'Praise the Lord,' and you say, Amen.'" If you did not join him in praising God, for he would always at once begin, he thought you were *dead*; "for is not," said he, "'the Lord worthy to be praised from the rising to the setting of the sun?' and yet you will not praise Him at all." But he determined if all other tongues were silent, that his should sing God's praise; if all other harps were hung upon the willows, that his should wake the sweetest music; and if all other hearts were dull and cold and hard, his should glow and flame with the fervour of devotion. He rightly thought that a *young prince of forty years of age*, as he used often to term himself, had abundant reason to rejoice. He was an adopted son of God, the "King of kings," and therefore he was a prince already possessing royal rights and privileges, and for him he exulted to think his Heavenly Father had reserved everlasting glory and blessedness.

I went with him one day to see a dying saint, whose character had been unblemished for many years, but whose natural disposition was modest and retiring almost to a fault. His face wore a look of ineffable dignity and repose, lit up with a strange, unearthly radiance and glory. He was just on the verge of heaven. He could only speak in a whisper. He said, "I wish I had a voice, so that I might praise the Lord!" "You should have praised Him, my brother, when you had one," was Billy's quiet, but slightly satirical comment.

> **SCRIPTURE TESTIMONY**
>
> *Death for the believer is to be with Christ*
>
> PHILIPPIANS 1:21-23 · I THES-
> SALONIANS 4:13

Billy's life was an almost perfect exemplification of the threefold injunction: "Rejoice evermore. —Pray without ceasing. —In everything give thanks." A Christian might be *poor*, but it was his duty to "rejoice evermore;" *afflicted*, but still he must "rejoice evermore;" *tempted* and *tried* and *persecuted*, but he must, notwithstanding, "rejoice evermore;" and surely this is divine heavenly wisdom, true Christian philosophy. Is there not a special blessing for the poor? Are they not often "rich in faith?" and has not God chosen them "heirs of the kingdom?" Ought not they then to rejoice? We all know that *affliction* is not "joyous, but grievous, nevertheless afterward it yieldeth the peaceable fruit of righteousness unto them which are exercised thereby." It is a *proof* of our Father's special love, and what is sufficient, if that is not, to cause us to rejoice? And we are expressly told that we are "to count it all joy when we fall into divers temptations." So did Billy Bray. He could smile through his tears. The sickness of a child, the death of a wife, were powerless to silence his voice, or to repress his joy. It is said that when his wife died he was so overpowered with the thought of his "dear Joey" having escaped from earth's toils and sufferings to the rest and bliss of heaven, that he began to jump and dance about the room, exclaiming, "Bless the Lord! My dear Joey is gone up with the bright ones! My dear Joey is gone up with the shining angels! Glory! Glory! Glory!" "Here," he would say, "we have a *little bitter*, but it is mixed with a *great deal of sweet*." Mr C. G. Honor, Primitive Methodist minister, says that at a love-feast in their chapel at St Blazey, when Billy was present, several persons spoke of their trials, but said that their blessings more than counterbalanced them. At length Billy rose; clapping his hands and smiling, he said, "Well, friends, I have been taking vinegar and honey, but, praise the Lord, I've had the vinegar with a *spoon*, and the honey with a *ladle*." He had trials as others, but "it was not worth while to speak or write anything about them." Was he not on the road to heaven, and why should not he praise God *every step of the way?* "I would rather *walk* to heaven," he has often said, "than ride to hell even in a fine carriage." But it excites a smile to hear him speak "of showing persons how we shall walk the golden streets in heaven, and with *golden slippers*, too." The death-chamber of many a "godly and devout" believer has been filled with his praises. Blessed use he has made of this incident in the life of the Rev. John Fletcher. Mrs F. says, "On Wednesday he told me he had received such a manifestation of the full meaning of those words, *God is love*, as he could never be able to express. 'It fills my heart,' said he, 'every moment. O Polly, my dear Polly, God is love! Shout! shout aloud! I want a gust of praise to go to the ends of the earth.'" Billy nearly always expressed a wish when he visited the sick and dying, that he might "see them in heaven, dressed in robes of glorious brightness; for," he would add, in his quietest vein of humour, "if I saw them there, *I must be there myself too.* They say that every man has got a little self, and so have I too, for

> 'I long to be there, His glory to share,
> And to lean on Jesus' breast.'"

If people said he praised God too "*loud,*" he would point heavenward and say, "Up there, we shall praise Him 'more sweet, more '*loud*;'" and sometimes, "If the Lord were to stop my breath this moment" (sudden death he used to call the fields' way to heaven), "I should be with Him in heaven at once. *I have a heaven while going to heaven.*"

"The men of grace have found glory begun below."

If any man could sing,

> "Heaven is my home,"

| SCRIPTURE TESTIMONY |
| :---: |
| *Whether we live or die, we are the Lord's* |
| ROMANS 14:7-8 |

it was Billy Bray. He said to a young friend on going to bed one night, "If you find me dead in the morning, mind you shout Hallelujah!" She told him she did not think it likely she should. "Why not?" he asked. "You might, for it would be all right." Blessed, blessed experience this! To be able to say truthfully, confidently, "For to me to live is Christ, and to die is gain," is certainly the highest privilege of men here; and this Billy could say always.

We may fitly close this chapter by the relation of two or three little incidents which illustrate the man and his character more fully than the most elaborate description could do.

In a friend's house, in Falmouth, he exhorted those present to praise the Lord. Speaking of himself, he said, "I can't help praising the Lord. As I go along the street I lift up one foot, and it seems to say, 'Glory!' and I lift up the other, and it seems to say 'Amen;' and so they keep on like that all the time I am walking."

Calling at a friend's house at a time when he had two or three visitors, he received a hearty welcome to remain and dine with them. He soon began to praise the Lord, which was as natural to him as for the birds to sing. He was asked if it was not possible for a man to get in the habit of praising the Lord without knowing what he was saying. He very coolly said *that he did not think the Lord was much troubled with that class of persons.*

On one occasion, when in the Penzance Circuit on special work, he slept with T. A. Very early in the morning Billy was out of bed, jumping, dancing, and singing the praises of God as usual. T. A. said, "Billy, why are you out thus so early? You will disturb the family, and perhaps give offence." The next moment Billy was again leaping and praising the Lord, and then, naming the members of the household and T. A., said, "They might lie and sleep and let their wheels get rusty if they liked, but he would see to it that his wheels were kept nicely oiled, and ready for work!" Then he fell on his knees and prayed aloud for the master and the mistress of the house and the members of the family, while his prayer for T. A. was that the *"Lord would have mercy on him, and make him a better man than he appears to be."*

When Mr Gilbert was in the St Austell Circuit the first time, Billy came to the anniversary of Tywardreath Highway Chapel. The chapel was so full that, when he came to the door, it was with difficulty he could get in; but he had no sooner uttered, in his own peculiar tone, the words, "Bless the Lord! little Billy Bray is come once more to Highway," than, as if by magic, a passage was made for him through the crowded audience. On reaching the pulpit he began to dance and shout because "little Billy Bray was again at Highway." He read the first line of the hymn beginning—

"Oh, for a thousand tongues to sing,"

and then said, "Just think, *that's nine hundred and ninety-nine more than I have got.* "Mr Gilbert says that he spent an hour or two with him in the evening. "I told him that I had seen his mother at Twelveheads, and that I found her in a very blessed frame of mind, and that whilst I was praying with her she became so happy that, although quite blind, she jumped and danced about the house, shouting the praises of God! Billy at once became much excited, and, rising from his chair, began to dance also. He then said, 'Dear old soul! dance, did she? I am glad to hear that. Bless the

Lord! Well, I dance sometimes. Why shouldn't I dance as well as David? David, you say, was a king; well, bless the Lord! I am a King's Son! I have as good a right to dance as David had. Bless the Lord! I get very happy at times; my soul gets full of the glory, and then I dance too! I was home in my chamber the other day, and I got so happy that I danced, and the glory came streaming down upon my soul, and it made me dance so lustily that my heels went down through the planchen.'"

Mr Gilbert adds: "When Billy was about to leave, in company with a youth who had come with him, he said, 'Johnny and I, we'll make the valleys ring with our singing and praising as we go home!' I said, ' Then you are a singer, Billy.' 'Oh yes, bless the Lord! I can sing. My heavenly Father likes to hear *me* sing. I can't sing so sweetly as some; but my Father likes to hear me sing as well as those who sing better than I can. My Father likes to hear the *crow* as well as the *nightingale*, for He made them both.'"

Mr Robins informs me that at a chapel anniversary he said at one time: "I went in to Truro to buy a frock for the little maid, and coming home I felt very happy, and got catching up my heels a little bit, and I danced the frock out of the basket. When I came home Joey said, 'William, where's the frock?' I said, 'I don't know, "es-en-a" in the basket?' 'No,' said Joey. 'Glory be to God,' I said, 'I danced the frock out of the basket.' The next morning I went to the class-meeting, and one was speaking of his trials, and another was speaking of his trials, and I said, 'I've got trials too, for yesterday I went into Truro, and bought a frock for the little maid. Coming home I got catching up my heels a little bit, and I danced the frock out of the basket.' So they gave me the money I had paid for the frock, and two or three days afterwards some one picked up the frock and brought it to me; so I had two frocks for one. Glory!" and he closed his narration with one of his favourite sayings when persons opposed and persecuted him for singing and shouting so much, "If they were to put me into a barrel, I would shout glory out through the bung-hole! Praise the Lord!"

The Rev. S. W. Christophers says that "the first time he saw and heard Billy, among other things he said was this: 'If Billy gets work, he praises the Lord; when he gets none, he sings all the same. Do'e think that He'll starve Billy? No, no, there's sure to be a bit of flour in the bottom of the barrel for Billy. I can trust in Jesus, and while I trust 'im, He'd as soon starve Michael the Archangel as He'd starve Billy!'

"The next time I heard that voice was when, to all human appearance, I was about to depart from this mortal life. The hallowed stillness of my bed-room was then broken by the distant sound of the well-known Hallelujah!' and then the jubilant tones of the faithful soul as he mounted the stairs singing —

> 'There, there, at His feet we shall suddenly meet.
> And be parted in body no more!
> We shall sing to our lyres, with the heavenly choirs.
> And our Saviour in glory adore!'

"I was raised up to see and hear Billy again, many, many times.

"I remember somebody saying to him as he sat at a friend's table, 'How long should I pray at a time to keep my soul healthy?' 'Do'e see that there piece of brass?' replied he, pointing to a polished ornament on the chimney-piece. ' If you give that five minutes rub every now and then you'll keep it bright; but if you let'im go a long time without it, you will have a long rub to get'im bright again'"

# CHAPTER IV.

## CHAPEL BUILDING.

*"Thou shalt arise, and have mercy upon Zion: for the time to favour*
*her, yea, the set time is come. For Thy servants take pleasure in*
*her stones, and favour the dust thereof." — Psalm 102:13, 14.*

P ROBABLY NO part of England is better supplied with places of religious worship than the county of Cornwall. The great majority of
these have been built by the self-denying efforts and liberality of
the poor rather than by the encouragement and munificence of persons
belonging to the wealthier classes. The power and efficacy of the voluntary
principle may be here witnessed in full operation on a large scale. The
people generally have put their "shoulder to the wheel," and have preferred
to help themselves to being dependent on the charity of others—they have
trusted almost wholly to God's blessing on their own exertions. "Methodism," as the late Bishop of Exeter told us, "is the mother-church of
Cornwall," and its different sections have a strong hold upon the affections
and sympathies of the population; and notwithstanding some defects of
character, and extravagances of worship—ignorantly or wickedly exagger-
ated by some High-Church writers—they are honourably distinguished
for their sobriety and intelligence, and, greater honour still, as a God-fear-
ing, Christ-loving, and Sabbath-keeping people. For this result we are
largely indebted to men of the Billy Bray type. This will be more evident

in subsequent chapters, but we have now to furnish some particulars of his early chapel-building enterprises, in which, as in all his actions, he sought to do his Master's will and promote His glory. Billy's own version of those occurrences, which are so widely known and so deeply interesting, is as follows:—

| SCRIPTURE TESTIMONY |
| --- |
| *God's work will not lack God's supply* |
| PHILIPPIANS 4:19 |

"In the neighbourhood where I lived there were a great many dark-minded, wicked people, and chapels were few. The Lord put it into my mind to build a chapel. My mother had a small place; and by one of her little fields there was a small piece of common. The Lord opened my mother's heart to give a spot on that piece of common to build on. When my mother gave me the ground, I began to work as the dear Lord told me, and to take away the hedge of my mother's field, and to dig out the foundation for a chapel, or a house to worship God in, which was to be called *Bethel*. Many will have to bless God for ever that Bethel Chapel was built, for many are in heaven already that were born there. In that day there was but one little chapel in our neighbourhood, at a place called Twelveheads, which belonged to the Wesleyans. Our people had a little old house to preach in, which would hold only twenty or thirty persons. So we wanted a place to preach in, and the people a place to hear in. Paul had a thorn in the flesh, and so had I. For I had not only the wicked against me; but a little class which was held in the house where we preached; most of them turned against me, and tried to set the preachers against me. But with all they could do, they could not hurt me, though they made me uneasy at times. When I had got out the foundation of the Lord's house, we had preaching on the foundation-stone. [Mr A. says that Billy, "standing on the stone, said, 'If this new chapel, which they say is to be called Bethel, stands one hundred years, and one soul be converted in it every year, that will be one hundred souls, and one soul is worth more than all Cornwall.' He then danced on the stone, and shouted 'Glory, glory, bless the Lord."] On the day that it was laid one of our neighbours said he would not give anything towards Billy Bray's chapel. He had two horses that drew the *whim* at the mine; one of them was taken lame in the field, and lost many days' work. Then the people said that the horse was taken lame because the owner would not give anything to Billy Bray's chapel. But the people must know that it was not mine, but the dear Lord's chapel. And it may be the Lord punished him for not giving anything to *His* chapel. But the chapel was never much good to that man, for he died very soon after; and the Lord enabled me to build the chapel without his help, bless and praise His holy name. When I had taken down the field hedge, cleared out the foundation, had got some stone home to the place where the chapel was to be built, when the masons had put up some of the walls, and I had 15s. given me by friends, the devil entered into some of my class-mates, who said that the chapel ought not to be built there; and when my class-mates saw that they could not stop me, they went to the superintendent of the circuit and told him that he ought to stop me from building the chapel there, for that was not the place, it ought to be built at *Twelveheads*, or at *Tippett's Stamps*. Our preacher came to me, and told me that the class had been to him to stop me from building the chapel where I had begun. Then I told him that the Lord had put it into my mind to build the chapel there, and I showed him what I had done already towards building the chapel. It was the preaching night; and he asked me whether I would be willing to cast lots whether the chapel should be built where I had begun it or in another place 'Yes,' I said, 'I was willing; for I did not want to build the chapel there unless it was the Lord's will.' In the evening we went to meeting and most of our little class were there, and the men who were against me. After preaching our preacher wrote three lots, for Twelve heads, Tippett's Stamps, and Cross Lattes, which was the place where I had begun my chapel. When they drew lots the lot came for Cross Lanes to be the place for the chapel. They then said they would help me to get on with it by raising stone; but telling about it that night was all they did to help me. The following day one of them came to me and said, 'We shall not help you, for Cross Lanes did not ought to be the lot.' So I was as well off as I thought I should be. I went to work, and raised stone, and got mortar, and set the masons to work. And the dear Lord helped me, for I was very poor, and had no money of my own. But the dear Lord raised me up friends, who sent me money to pay the masons; we got the chapel walls up, and timber for the roof; and then got it sawed and put up. But we had not timber enough by one principal; and I asked my Heavenly Father to send me some timber, or money to buy some. That morning there was a Wesleyan local preacher home praying; the Lord said to him while he was on his knees, 'Go down and give William Bray a pound note.' At that time there were no sovereigns; there were one pound notes, drawn on the banks. After he had taken his breakfast he came down to me by the chapel, and said to me, 'What do you want a pound note for?' and I replied, 'To buy timber to put a principal up on that end of the chapel.' He said he never felt such a thing in all his life, 'for while I was home praying this morning it was always coming into my mind to go down and give you a pound note, and here it is.'

| SCRIPTURE TESTIMONY |
| :---: |
| *God answers prayer* |
| LUKE 18:7 · JOHN 15:7 · ACTS 12:5 · JAMES 5:15 |

So I had the note, went to Truro, bought a principal, put it up on the chapel, and there it is to this day. When the timber was on the chapel, I went round, and got two pounds towards covering the chapel. At that time we had young children, and the youngest of them was taken very ill. When my little maid was taken ill, Satan tempted me that it would take seven pounds to cover the chapel, and I had but two pounds; and our little one would die, and it would take one pound to bury her, and then I should have but one pound left. The devil tempted me very much on that point; for if I wanted it I had a right to take it, for the dear Lord and 'me' in this place kept but one purse;[1] and I paid any money that I earned at mine to the chapel, when I wanted it. So I had but one to give my account to, and that was the dear Lord, the very best comrade that man can ever have. So the devil tempted me that the child would die. While I was thus sore tempted, it came into my mind that I should be paid for building this chapel, and it was applied to me, 'Because thou hast built this chapel, I will save thy child's life.' And I said, 'Where is this coming from?' And it was said to me, 'I am the God of Abraham, Isaac, and Jacob, be nothing doubting, it

---

1   This expression may be misunderstood without an explanation. He freely used his own money, when he had any, but what was given him for the Lord's cause was sacredly appropriated.

is I, saith the Lord;' and I believed it; and it was so. When I went home I told my wife that the child would not die, for the Lord had told me so. She replied, 'Don't say so; for all the neighbours say she will die, she is so very ill.' I then went to the mine to work; when I came home the child was not any better, and had not eaten any meat. On that night the child was very ill; and got no better all the forenoon of the next day. She was very ill when I came home to dinner. That day I was afternoon 'core' at the mine; and ever since the Lord converted my soul I always felt it my duty to pray with my wife and children before leaving my home to go to work. We knelt down to pray; the child was lying in the window-seat; we had for dinner what was very plentiful at that time, fish and potatoes; and in my prayer I said, 'Dear Lord, thou hast said that my child shall live, but she has not eaten any meat yet. ' And she began to eat meat there and then. She is living now, and is the mother of ten children; so the Lord made the devil a liar once more. The devil did not do me any hurt; he only made me bolder. I had only two pounds; and the cost would be seven pounds by the time the roof was on. I borrowed a horse, and rode ten or twelve miles from where I lived, up among the farmers, and asked one of them whether he had any reed to sell, for I wanted three hundred sheaves. He told me he had, and that it was £2 for a hundred. So I told the farmer to bring three hundred sheaves to me as soon as he could, and some spears for them. But I did not tell him that I had only two pounds. He brought down one hundred first, and some spears. I had three pounds when he came; so I paid him for the hundred of reed, and the spears; and had a few shillings left. I asked the farmer to bring down the rest of the reed as soon as he could; but didn't tell him I had not money to pay for it. And in wasn't necessary that I should, for by the time the other two hundred sheaves were sent a friend gave me money to pay for it. Then I put a man to work to cover the roof, and that would cost one pound ten shillings with a little other work besides; and when the man came to be paid I had but one pound; so I wanted ten shillings more. The Lord put it into my mind to go into a high road near where a great many people went up and down to work; and the first man I met was P. B. I said to him, 'You have not given me anything yet towards my Father's house? And he said, 'No;

nor do I intend to.' I replied, 'What, are you "amind" for the Lord to say
to you *in that* day, 'You saw me hungred, and gave me no meat, thirsty,
and ye gave me no drink; a stranger, and ye took me not in; naked, and
ye clothed me not?' And he said, 'Well, I don't mind if I do give you ten
shillings.' I said, 'That is just the money I want.' So he gave me the ten
shillings; and I went home and paid the thatcher.

"After that I wanted timber for the door and windows and forms. A
mine had lately stopped; and they were selling off the timber. There was
a bargain in timber, for one pound six shillings; but I had not money to
buy it. To a friend who asked me whether I had been to the mine, and
bought any timber, I said I had not, because I had no money. Then he
gave me one pound, and with that and some other sums the Lord sent
me from other places I was able to buy what I wanted. As the timber
had to be brought home to the dear Lord's house, I wanted a horse and
cart. One of our neighbours had a horse, but he said she would not draw
anything. I asked him to lend her to me. He told me I might have her,
but she would not draw; but I took the mare and put her in the cart, and
brought the timber home. I never saw a better horse in my life; I did not
touch her with whip or stick, though we had steep hills to come up over.
When I took back the mare, and told my neighbour, 'I never saw a better
mare,' he said, 'I never saw such a thing; she will not draw with any one
else.' That mare was working that day for a very strong company, Father,
Son, and Holy Ghost; horses, angels, men, and devils must obey them.
If there had been no one there more powerful than Billy Bray, she would
have been as bad with him as with anybody else. But, bless and praise the
name of the dear Lord, He said, 'The horse shall work, for the timber is
to seat my house' and what the dear Lord says shall be obeyed.

"I went on and finished the chapel. Then some of them said, 'Now your
chapel is done, you shall not have preaching there.' When they said that,
I locked up the chapel door, and carried the key home, and hung it to a
nail behind the door. I said, 'Lord, there is the key; I have done what Thou
hast told me to do; the chapel is built, and there is the key; if it is Thy will
the key should stay there seven years, or that it should be taken down
every minute in the day, Thy will be done, my dear Lord.' That very day

our preacher appointed services at the new chapel even more frequently than I should have asked had I been present. They named my chapel *Bethel*. We had preaching there every Sabbath, afternoon and evening, and class-meeting in the morning. The Lord soon revived His work, and we gathered a great many members. A large new chapel has been built since near the old one, which has also taken the name of 'Bethel.' The old one is now used as a school-house, and for class-meetings. No wonder that the devil was so against me while I was building the old *Bethel*, and put his servants to hinder me, for I have seen at one time fifty down asking for mercy, and mercy they had.

"A little while after I had done building Bethel Chapel the Lord said to me, 'I have made you instrumental in building Bethel

| SCRIPTURE TESTIMONY |
| :---: |
| *Fervently and zealously serve the Lord* |
| ROMANS 12:11 |

Chapel, and I will make you the instrument in building one at *Kerley Downs*.' When this was applied to me I believed it, and rejoiced greatly to think that I was honoured to work for so good a Master as the King of heaven, and earth, and sky. Kerley Downs was near a mile from

*Kerley Downs Chapel.*

where I lived, in the same parish. At this place there was preaching in a dwelling-house, and a class met in the same house. The friends had been trying for some time to get a spot for a chapel, but had been disappointed. They had made a collection for the chapel they intended to have, but the site was sold to a man for a higher price after it had been promised to the society. One of the neighbours who owned a farm said to one of the class, 'Where is the money you collected so long ago towards a chapel? Which you have not begun yet.' He said, 'If you have a mind to build a chapel, you may have ground of me.' I told the preacher we could have a spot for a chapel, and if he did not call a meeting to appoint trustees I should begin about the chapel myself. So he appointed a day and got trustees; but all that promised to help left me to myself. So my little son and me went to work, and got some stone; the good friend who gave the land lent me his horse and cart; and we soon set the masons to work. Those who read this must remember that I was a very poor man, with a wife and five small children at that time, and worked in the mine underground. Sometimes I was forenoon 'core,' and when I had taken my dinner I should go to the chapel and work as long as I could see, and the next day do the same. The next week I should be afternoon 'core; ' then I should go up to the chapel in the morning and work until the middle of the day, and then go home and away to the mine. The week following I should be night 'core;' I should then work about the chapel by day, and go to mine by night; and had not the dear Lord greatly strengthened me for the work, I could not have done it. When I was about the chapel, I had potatoes to till in my garden; and every Sunday I was 'planned.' Sometimes I had to walk twenty miles, or more, and speak three times. I have worked twenty hours in the twenty-four; and had not the Lord helped me I could not have done it. Bless and praise His holy name, 'for in the Lord Jehovah is everlasting strength.' I do know He is a friend when all other friends leave us; and He will help us to overcome our enemies.

"When our chapel was up about to the door-head the devil said to me, 'They are all gone and left you and the chapel, and I would go and leave the place too.' Then I said, 'Devil, doesn't thee know me better than that;

by the help of the Lord I will have the chapel up, or lose my skin on the down.' So the devil said no more to me on that subject. Sometimes I have had blisters on my hands, and they have been very sore. But I did not mind that, for if the chapel should stand one hundred years, and if one soul were converted in it every year, *that* would be a hundred souls, and that would pay me well if I got to heaven, for they that 'turn many to righteousness shall shine as the stars for ever and ever.' So I thought I should be rich enough when I got there. The chapel was finished after a time: and the opening day came. We had preaching, but the preacher was a wise man, and a dead man. I believe there was not much good done that day, for it was a very dead time with preacher and people; for he had a great deal of *grammar*, and but little of *Father*. 'It is not by might, nor by power, but by my Spirit, saith the Lord.' If it was by wisdom or might, I should have but a small part, for my might is little and my wisdom less. Thanks be to God, the work is His, and He can work by whomsoever He pleases. The second Sunday after the chapel was opened I was 'planned' there. I said to the people, 'You know I did not work here about this chapel in order to fill my pocket, but for the good of the neighbours, and the good of souls; and souls I must have, and souls I will have.' The Lord blessed us in a wonderful manner. Two women cried to the Lord for mercy; then I said, 'Now the chapel is paid for already.' The dear Lord went on to work there; and the society soon went up from fifteen members to thirty. You see how good the Lord is to me; I spoke for one soul a year, and he gave me fifteen souls the first year, Bless and praise His holy name, for He is good, and His mercy endureth for ever, for one soul is worth a thousand worlds. Our little chapel had three windows, one on one side, and two on the other: the old devil, who does not like chapels, put his servants by way of reproach to call our chapel *Three-Eyes*. But, blessed be God, since then, the chapel has become too small for the place, and it has been enlarged; now there are six windows instead of three; and they may call the chapel Six-Eyes now if they will. For, glory be to God, many that have been converted there are now in heaven. And when we get there we will praise Him with all our might; and *he shall never hear the last of it.*

SCRIPTURE TESTIMONY

*God using an inner voice
to communicate*

JOHN 14:26 · ACTS 10:19-20 · ACTS 11:12

"After this the Lord led me to build another chapel in the parish of *Gwennap*. The Lord put it into the heart of a gentleman to grant me a piece of land; and after we had dug out the foundation, we wanted stone to build with. The Lord put it into my heart to go down by the railway and try to raise stone. Some one had been there before, and their quarry was poor. They had worked to the east and to the west, and left a piece of ground untouched in the middle. We went to work on this piece, and the dear Lord helped me, as He said. Some wondered to see what a lot of stone we got out. But they must know I was working for a strong company, the Father, Son, and Holy Ghost, and that company will never break. I worked in my 'core ' at the mine all the while I was raising stone; and as I was living a great way from the place where I was building the chapel, the Lord helped me again by putting it into a gentleman's heart to give me five shillings a month while I was raising stone for the dear Lord's house; at a coffee-house near the quarry, when I came up from mine last 'core' by night, I had my breakfast for sixpence or sevenpence, and then away to raise stone. When the masons were set to work, I had no money in hand, and no bank to go to but the bank heaven. But, thanks be to God, that is a *strong* bank; and I had often to go there by faith. At this time the Lord sent Mr T. to me, who said, 'You will want timber, and lime, and slate, will you not?' I said, 'Yes, sir.' Then he told me to go to his stores, and have what I wanted. When the masons wanted money I went round collecting, and the friends were very kind and gave me money. I went to Camborne, and farther west. Amongst other places I went to Helston, where there lived a miser said to be worth a great deal of money, who was never known to give anything to any object. When I asked him for something for the chapel, he said he could not afford to give me anything. I said, 'You can give me some money if you like, and if you do not you may soon die, *and leave it all behind.* Job was very rich, but he soon became poor. I am begging for the Lord's house, and if you do not give me something the Lord may take you away from your money, or your money away from you.' When I told him further that the gold was the Lord's, he said, ' Go round the town and see what you can get, and come to me again by and by.' I said to him, 'No, you have got money, and I must have some now,' and talked to him about what the Lord would do with *greedy* people. Then he wiped his mouth, put his hand into his pocket four or five times and talked away, but at last he took out two shillings and sixpence, and gave me. It was a hard job to get even that from the old miser. I do not think Satan let him sleep that night because the dear Lord permitted me to take half-a-crown from his god. When I told some of the friends that I had got half-a-crown from him, they said 'it was the greatest miracle ever performed in Helston.' I had a 'plan' at St Just, and after I had done my work there I went on to St Ives, and was directed to find out a good man named *Bryant*. St Ives was a small place about the year 1838. Friend Bryant told me that I had come to St Ives at a very poor time, for there was but little fish caught that year; and some of the people were almost wanting bread. 'It was poor times, ' I said, 'with Peter when the Lord told him to let down the net on the other side of the ship.' Br. Bryant missed, for I had come at a very good time, as the event proved. We went up to the Wesleyan Chapel; there were a great many lively members and we had a good meeting. We prayed to the dear Lord *to send some fish*, and He *did*. After the meeting was over, we went into a coffee-house to get a little refreshment; then we began our meeting, and continued it till *midnight*, praying to the Lord to *send in the fish*. As we came out of the meeting to go to our lodging, there were the dear, poor women with the pilchards on their plates, and the fish was shining in the moonlight. The women were smiling, the moon was smiling, and we were smiling; and no wonder, for the dear Lord put bread on many shelves that night, and blessed many families. We asked the women what fish was taken, and they told us that many boats had taken ten thousand, and some twenty thousand. Against the next day there were, if I mistake not, eight thousand casks taken. And here I must speak it to their credit, though the people had so many fish, and were so poor, they rested on Sunday, and left it till Monday before they went about their fish, *and they lost none*. Some of the fishermen said to me, '*Now you shall have some money for your chapel*; and if you will get a boat and come out we will give you some fish.' A friend with me, a carpenter, a bit used to the sea, got a boat and rowed me to the place where the fish were. They looked 'pretty,' for they were shining and leaping about, and the fishermen dipped up the fish and threw them into our boat I thought of the church-ministers, who took their *tithe* of the corn; but I took mine of the fish. When we came to land, the carpenter 'told' up the fish to the people that bought them, and I took the money, which amounted to £6.15s.

"A druggist, also, promised me the profits of one week on medicine sold, which brought me two guineas more. Altogether I brought away from St Ives £17 towards the chapel. So when I came home I could easily pay the masons and carpenters. You see how the Lord helped me through all, —first by putting it into a gentleman's heart to let me have a spot to build on; then to get good stone in what had been only a poor quarry; also in sending Mr T. to tell me, when I was not worth a penny, to go to his store for timber and lime and slate; then in enabling me to collect so much towards the expense of building; and particularly at St Ives, when the dear Lord sent the fish in answer to prayer. He has said, 'Call upon me in the day of trouble, and I will deliver thee, and thou shalt glorify me.' And we are 'in everything by prayer and supplication with thanksgiving to let our requests be made known unto God.' Bless His holy name: I will praise Him and glorify Him for ever and ever. 'O magnify the Lord with me, and let us exalt His name together. I sought the Lord, and He heard me, and delivered me from all my fears.... This poor man cried, and the Lord heard him, and saved him out of all his troubles.'"

Many further interesting particulars respecting Billy Bray's chapels might be given, but which we must mostly omit. The details of one circumstance, briefly referred to by Billy, we may append. One account I have received speaks of Billy calling on a Mr T., a liberal gentleman well known in the neighbourhood, but Billy speaks of the Lord having "sent" Mr T. to him. Billy told the gentleman that he was going "to build a 'fishing-net' near Carharrack, in order to catch the fine fish that might be found in such large shoals in the neighbourhood." Mr T. was so well pleased with the simplicity and earnestness of Billy, that he said, "So, Billy, you are going to build a 'fishing-net,' are you? I understand by that, that you are going to build a chapel; now when you have succeeded in getting up the walls

*Great Deliverance Chapel.*

sufficiently high to take the roof, let me know, and I will at once take steps to give a roof to your 'fishing-net.'" "Bless the Lord," was Billy's response, and the same moment he was jumping and dancing for joy! When Mr T. was told that the "fishing-net" required a roof, he said he would see it to know what was wanted. On reaching the spot, he expressed his surprise that so large a chapel had been built, intimating that when he made the promise he had no idea that Billy intended to erect such a large "fishing-net." His answer was, "Bless the Lord! my Heavenly Father deserves a large house." Mr T. cheerfully fulfilled his promise, and the "fishing-net" was soon adorned with a roof. The gentleman afterwards became a worshipper in "Great Deliverance" Chapel (the name it received, and by which it is still known), and a valuable member and class-leader.

SCRIPTURE TESTIMONY

*Ask Me anything in My name*

MATTHEW 18:19 · JOHN 14:13-14 · JOHN 16:23-24

When Billy was building his first chapel, some of his friends, whose faith was not so strong as his own, told him he had better build it with a chimney, so that it could be turned more easily into a cottage if it did not answer as a chapel. "No," he said, "I will have no chimney in it, except it be to drive the devil out through," though we fear a chimney would be but of little use for that purpose.

When the little place at Kerley Downs was up, Billy began to think where the pulpit could come from. At last, as he looked about among some furniture at an auction sale, his eye fell upon an old three-cornered cupboard.

"The very thing," cried Billy, "the very thing. I can cut a slit down the back of un, and strengthen the middle of un, and put a board up in front of un, and clap a pair o' steers behind un, and then the preacher can preach out of un pretty."

With much glee he turned to some one near him, and asked, "What do'e think they'll want for that there cup board?" The man looked, and gave it as his opinion that it would go for six shillings. Billy told him what he meant to do with it, and the man said—"Why, you're Billy Bray. Here, I'll give'e the six shilling to buy it."

After a while the cupboard was put up. Billy knew nothing of auctions. All eager to have his pulpit, he cried, holding out his hand—"Here, Mister Auctineer, here's six shillin' for un, I do want un for a pulpit."

Of course there was a great laugh at Billy's expense. As it passed away the auctioneer cried—"Six shillings, going for six." A nod from behind Billy was quickly caught. "Seven," said the auctioneer, "seven shillings."

"No," cried Billy, "'tis on'y six, there's the money."

Of course, down went the hammer, and much to Billy's astonishment the cupboard was not his.

"Well, Father do know best," said he, in a rather disappointed tone; "but anyhow I must give the man back his six shilling."

The man was gone, nor was Billy likely to see him again. This was a new and even greater trouble.

"I'll be gone down an' tell Father about it," said Billy, as he started off for his little chapel.

With faith renewed, and a comfortable assurance that it would be all right, he was coming from the chapel when he saw the cupboard going up the hill in a cart.

"I'll follow un, anyhow," he whispered, "an' see the end." They carried it to a house, and tried to take it inside, but it was just too big to get in. They twisted and turned, they pulled and pushed, but it was no use.

Here's a mess," said the purchaser, angrily; "I've given seven shilling for en, an' shall have to skat en up for firewood."

Then as his eyes twinkled, Billy stepped over and put his hand on the man's shoulder as he stood, hat in hand, wiping his forehead.

"I'll give'e six shillin' for un, if you'll carry un down to my little chapel."

"That I will," said the man, pleased at being so well out of it.

"*Bless the Lord*" cried Billy, "'*tis just like Him. He knew I couldn' carry en myself so He got this man to carry en for me.*"[1]

This chapter reads almost like a romance; but the devout reader will clearly see God's hand in the matters related, and that His chosen instrument was eminently qualified to carry out His purpose. The fitting of means to ends has as remarkable illustrations in Providence as in Creation. That same divine wisdom which chose Luther to be the hero of the Reformation, and Wesley and Whitfield to rouse a slumbering church and nation from their spiritual lethargy, and Livingstone to be the pioneer of the Gospel in interior Africa, endued Billy Bray with all the needful qualifications "to serve his generation according to the will of God" in the way described in this chapter. The Lord made abundant use of his tact and cheerfulness, because wholly devoted to Him. He succeeded therefore where others have failed, and brought discredit upon themselves and their friends. Thus when Billy appealed in one instance for a second subscription in behalf of "Great Deliverance" Chapel, the gentleman met him by the objection that he had subscribed to that chapel once before. "Yes," Billy said, "but how many deeces of wool have you had since then?" Nothing more was said, but a donation was at once handed to the "wise" beggar. The success of a man whose temper is never a fault, and whose wit turns everything to good account, is certain. A friend who was with Billy on a begging expedition, suggested, as they were coming near a gentleman's house, and Billy was evidently making for the front door, that it would be better if they went to the back door. "No," said Billy, "I am the son of a

---

1   This graphic description is from the pen of the Rev. M. G Penson

King, and I shall go frontways." And then his motives were above suspicion, and his faith in God was of the strongest kind. His own words are: "I have no more fear of the Lord bringing me right out and right through than if this road was covered with gold; for His word is as good as ready money."

We may and we do admire Billy's simplicity and persistency of purpose, but his inward satisfaction none can share. We get many glimpses of it, but we must content ourselves with the briefest reference thereto. When he was got an old man, and had forgotten perhaps many of the exploits of his younger days, he heard in a public meeting, many miles from his home, a person speak of a man who had been instrumental in building several chapels in which many had been converted, and in one of which he, the speaker, had been a Sunday scholar. Billy was listening with interest to this recital, quite unconscious that he was the person meant, but when his name was mentioned his heart leaped for joy that he had been permitted to do some good; that he had persevered though the people did say that Billy was silly; that the Lord had sent many wise men to preach in the chapels which silly Billy Bray had built; that though he was only a rams horn, the Lord had given His people some silver trumpets; that many were in heaven who had been converted in these chapels; and above all did he rejoice that his dear Lord was the great master-builder, to whom all the praise belonged.

# CHAPTER V.

## THE PRAYER OF FAITH.

*"And the prayer of faith shall save the sick,*
*and the Lord shall raise him up." — James 5:15.*

A FEW YEARS ago there were "strange reports of wonderful cures wrought in a remote Swiss village by a Christian woman. . . . Wonders are out of date in the

nineteenth century; there is a natural incredulity of everything like miracle, and the stories came and went, were told and ridiculed, and dropped from year to year. Yet any one having the curiosity to visit the "pretty" village of Mannedorf would have been well repaid; "for there lived Dorothea Trudel, who was characterised after her conversion" by great earnestness, by singularly profound spiritual knowledge, and by a quiet, happy, and modest Christian spirit. She was a worker in flowers, and came, in time, to have workers under her; and when she was about thirty-seven, four or five of her workers fell sick. The sickness resisted all treatment, grew worse, appeared to be hopeless. She was a diligent and unselfish nurse, and as a Christian her anxiety for the work-people drove her to earnest prayer and careful consideration of the Scriptures. It was during this period that, like a sudden light, she says the well-known passage from James 5:14, 15, flashed

49

upon her. If medical skill was unavailing, was there not prayer? And could not the same Lord who chose to heal through medicines, also heal without them? Was He necessarily restricted to the one means? There was a time when His healing power went forth directly; might it not be put forth directly still? The doctors were at fault; but was not faith in God perhaps more at fault? Agitated by these questions, she sought help in prayer. And then kneeling by the bedsides of these sick people, she prayed for them. They recovered; and the thought that at first had startled her, became now the settled conviction of her life. A sickness broke out in the village, and where it did break out, her help, tenderness, and Christian teaching were rarely absent. She sought the recovery of the patients in answer to prayer alone. Many got better; and as the rumour spread, persons from the neighbourhood came or sent, and her leisure was fully occupied.

"Meanwhile she had resisted all solicitations to leave her ordinary work, and establish a kind of cure. Her proper calling, she considered, was the one which God had provided for her—that of a worker in flowers; her natural shyness and reserve made her shrink from publicity; but as increased numbers came and even besieged her doors, she was compelled to reconsider her position, and at last, with much reluctance, to receive persons into her house. This was at first out of mere compassion, when the sick had been brought from a distance and could find no proper shelter or care if she turned them away. By degrees the one house grew into three, and her days were spent in superintendence and in constant prayer; patients came from France and Germany, an even Great Britain. There came to be, in fact, an hospital at Männedorf." And in this work she continued until her death; and whatever judgment may be passed upon it, as the able writer says from whom we have quoted, "it is worth record as a feature of the Christian life of our century. Nor is it solitary, others are reported working similarly in other parts of Switzerland. Pastor Blumhardt of Wurtemberg has had his house crowded with patients for years. Dr Bushnell in his 'Nature and the Supernatural,' reports like instances from America. There is no supposition of fraud. Will mesmerism, animal magnetism, the power of sympathy, be adequate explanation? Or is there still a prayer of faith that shall save the sick, and the Lord shall raise him up?"

That there is danger of this principle being perverted and dishonoured, the "doings" of the "Peculiar People" are sufficient evidence. The slightest approach to extravagance and fanaticism ought to be carefully guarded against; and even the method adopted by our Lord when He wrought miracles for the relief of suffering men during His brief sojourn upon earth teaches the same lesson. Nature itself is a great dispensary where God has treasured up His remedies for all diseases "which flesh is heir to," which are discoverable by patient and prayerful study, and which is a sufficient indication of His will and general method of working. But then, has He so tied Himself up to merely natural laws and processes that He has only one way of working left, only one way of healing His children? This would be to make "law" supreme and inexorable, and to concede what sceptical philosophers have always demanded—viz., that a miracle being contrary to the course and constitution of nature is clearly impossible.

So much in explanation of certain facts in Billy Bray's life which we could not entirely pass over, and which, in fact, we gladly and gratefully record to the honour of Him whose Providence never fails, whose Wisdom is never baffled, and whose Power and Goodness can never be exhausted.

"I am about," says Billy, "to write of a woman in whom God's power was made manifest in a wonderful manner. I had the account from her own lips twice, and I will write

> SCRIPTURE TESTIMONY
>
> *God gave signs and wonders through the apostles*
>
> ACTS 5:12

down as near as I can what she told me. *Florence Hoskin,* for that was her name, was made a cripple by the ill-usage of one of her family, and wholly lost the use of one of her legs for seven years, and she was obliged to go on a crutch and stick. She was so weak that she was forced to drag her foot after her; and the doctor told her she would not have the use of her leg any more. But he made a mistake, for she was made sound again; our God is a God of all power, and there is nothing too great for Him to do. She was old when she was converted. In 1844, I think the Saturday night before the first Sunday in July, she went to bed greatly cast down. She prayed to her dear Lord, who is able to heal both body and soul; and that sister Hoskin soon found to her joy and satisfaction. She prayed away until the cloud broke from her mind, and she was made very happy in the love of Jesus. Then she said, 'Now, my dear Lord, Thou hast healed my soul, why not heal my body too?' She meant her lame leg; and when she said so, the Lord said to her, 'Arise, and go down to the Gospel-house, and there thou shalt be healed.' Then she said, 'Why not be healed here, my dear Lord?' for she was in bed, and it was an easy place for a poor cripple. When she said so, the Lord's Spirit was taken away from her. Then she said, 'I will go to Thy Gospel-house, or anywhere else, only let me be healed, my dear Lord.' Her Lord said to her, 'If I heal thee here, they will not believe it, for there are many of them as unbelieving as the Jews were in Jerusalem.' And if the dear Lord had healed her in the bed, many would have doubted; there are many unbelieving people in our country, and it is hard to make them believe. The Lord told sister Hoskin to go to the chapel, so that there should be many witnesses of His mighty power in healing her. It was on a Sunday that she rose out of her bed to go to the Gospel-house to get healed, strong in faith; but when she got down-stairs it was as if the devil stood in the door-way, to tempt her to have her breakfast first; but she said, 'No, devil, I will not, for thou hast many times tempted me to stay for breakfast, and I have had a dead meeting through being so late.' So she left home with her crutch and stick, and went away to her Gospel-house, dragging her poor lame foot on the ground. When she came to the chapel it was so early that there was no one there. When her leader came, he said, 'How is it you are down here so early to-day, Florence?' She said to him, 'Great things are going to be done here to-day; I am going to have a sound leg, for the dear Lord has told me so.' Her class-leader told her he thought she was mad; he said to her, 'If she had not more faith than he had, she never would be cured of her lameness.' So the meeting began; and while one was praying, Florence said, 'Pray away, the balm is coming.' She had faith to believe, and when the meeting was over she could walk about the chapel without crutch or stick. Some of the people that saw her walking about the chapel at Porthleven, went round the little town and said, Florence Hoskin is walking about the 'Bryanites" chapel without a crutch or stick. A great many came together to see what a miracle the dear Lord had wrought. As she was going out of the chapel, one person said,

'Here, Florence, is your crutch and stick,' when she answered, 'You may have them if you will, for I shall not want them any more.' And she did not want crutch or stick any more while she lived. Some foolish people will say, 'The Lord does not work miracles in these days as in the days of old.' The dear Lord does; if we can believe. Florence Hoskin believed; and according to her faith it was done unto her, for she went away from her home a cripple, and in a few hours came back healed: so it was well for her that she served the Lord. Bless and praise His name for ever."

Here is another case, as late as February 1865: —

"I went to *Kestle Mill* (to a Wesleyan Chapel to hold a teetotal meeting), a place some miles from Newlyn. A man who lived in Newlyn, called 'grandfather,' who

| SCRIPTURE TESTIMONY |
| :---: |
| *According to your faith* |
| *be it done to you* |
| MATTHEW 9:27-31 |

was very *lame*, wished to go with me; but when we had gone a little way he said he was so lame that he should not be able to go on. I said to him, 'You must go; Father must heal you.' He was going very lame when I said this; it was a great pain for him to walk. So I looked up to heaven, and prayed, and said, 'My dear Father, heal him;' and the dear Lord made him a sound man. He said, 'All my pain is gone;' and he went on to Kestle Mill as fast as I could go. When we came to the place 'grandfather' gave out a hymn and prayed; then he told the people what a bad drunkard he had been; but he was a teetotaler now, the Lord had converted his soul, and he was a happy man. When grandfather had done speaking, I spoke. *Twenty* signed the pledge. Then we travelled home; but I heard no more about his pain. On the Tuesday we had a teetotal meeting at our chapel in Newlyn, several Wesleyans on the platform. On Thursday, the 16th, after I had spoken in the Wesleyan Chapel at Newlyn, 'grandfather' rose from his seat, and told all the people in the chapel how that he was almost a cripple last week, and how that the dear Lord had healed him at once on Monday while going to Kestle Mill, and that he had not felt any pain since."

Billy also speaks of a brother Hicks who "had been in bed seven years, and was two years without speech, whom the Lord brought out in one day;" whose cure was wrought when a good brother resolved that "he would not cease praying for him until he could speak." Billy's faith was unquestioning in the power and willingness of that Saviour who "is in every place and age the same."

This is still more characteristic. At one time he had a child seriously ill, and his wife feared it would die. She wished Billy to go to the doctor, and get some medicine. He took eighteenpence in his pocket, all the money there was in the house. On the road he met a man who had lost a cow, and was then out begging for money to buy another, whose story touched Billy's heart, and to him the money was at once given. He said afterwards, "I felt after I had given away the money that it was no use to go to the doctor, for I could not have medicine without money, so I thought I would tell Father about it. I jumped over a hedge, and while telling the Lord all about it, I felt sure the 'cheeld' would live. I then went home, and as I entered the door, said to my wife, 'Joey, the cheeld's better, isn't it?' 'Yes,' she said. 'The cheeld will live, the Lord has told me so,'" was his answer, and the child soon got well.

But if these were the somewhat rare and more remarkable fruits of a faith which "staggered not at the promise of God through unbelief," it was ever in active operation, always made him happy and contented with his lot, saved him from all anxious care, and diffused over the whole of his life a heavenly radiance, some of the rays of which fell upon others wherever he went. The deep wisdom of the principles he had adopted possibly he did not know himself, but of their reality and blessedness he was fully conscious. How beautiful, how instructive, showing how far Billy was removed from fanaticism, is the following:—

"My wife said to me one day when lying on her sickbed, 'William, I do not see anything from heaven.' Neither do I, and what need has the Lord to show us sights,' ["Except ye see signs and wonders, ye will not believe," our Lord said to "a certain nobleman, whose son was sick at Capernaum "] 'when we can believe without it?'" He continued: "If I saw the Saviour a babe in the manger, I should not believe it more than I do now. If I saw Him raise Lazarus out of the grave, I should not believe it more than I do now. If I saw the Lord Jesus raise the ruler's daughter or the widow's son to life, I should not believe it more than I do now. And if I saw the dear

Lord nailed to the cross, and heard Him cry, 'It is finished,' saw Him give up the ghost, and rise from the tomb the third day, I should not believe these things more than I do now." When he said this his wife exclaimed, "And so do I believe it," and they greatly rejoiced together.

This simple faith in God and in His Word, what wonders it can accomplish. It is the "secret of power." It is a choice and powerful weapon in the Christian's armoury, which can be used at all times, and never fails. But in dealing with the sick and ignorant it has a special value. Billy speaks of an old man, who had been very wicked, but who was seeking mercy. His visitor said to him, "You need not fear, for if you ask the Lord for it you are sure to find it. It is said, 'Let the heart of him rejoice that seeketh the Lord,' for they that seek are sure to find Him, and when you have found Him you will have a good prize." But the old man did not at once get the blessing, and so Billy continued: "Suppose that you were very poor, and you knew that there was a bag of money in this room, and you were sure that if you sought for it you would find it, and that it would supply all your wants, and you would never be poor any more; then you would search the room with a *good heart*. The Lord is here, and when you find Him you will have all you want." As this was said, the old man sprung from his seat, exclaiming, "I have got it!" His wife heard him, ran into the room, fell on his neck, both rejoicing exceedingly in the God of their salvation. The old man said, "I never felt anything so 'pretty' in all my life." But how much he lost, is Billy's reflection, because he did not begin to serve God before. This incident reminds us of another characteristic feature of our friend's life, but which may very appropriately be dwelt on, more at length, in our next chapter.

# CHAPTER VI.

## PURE RELIGION.

*"Then shall the King say unto them on His right hand, Come, ye blessed of my Father, inherit the kingdom prepared for you from the foundation of the world: for I was an hungred, and ye gave me meat: I was thirsty, and ye gave me drink: I was a stranger, and ye took me in: naked, and ye clothed me: I was sick, and ye visited me: I was in prison, and ye came unto me.... Verily I say unto you, Inasmuch as ye have done it unto one of the least of these my brethren ye have done it unto me." — Matthew 25:34-30, 40.*

I N THIS memorable Scripture, we are taught that the humblest disciples—the poor, the sick, the despised —are more precious unto their Divine Lord than is light to the eye, or music to the ear, or knowledge to the mind, or love to the heart. He so fully identifies Himself with His people, that an injury done to them He reckons as an injury done to Him, while a blessing bestowed upon them is a blessing bestowed upon Him. It is no wonder, therefore, that the Apostle James should declare that "*pure religion* and undefiled before God and the Father is this, To visit the fatherless and widows in their affliction, and to keep himself unspotted from the world." These two distinct parts of "pure religion" may be said to be equal in importance,

> **SCRIPTURE TESTIMONY**
>
> *Generously give to those in need*
>
> ACTS 4:32-37 · GALATIANS 6:2 · HEBREWS 13:16 · I JOHN 3:17

but it is to the first part—visiting the fatherless and widows in their affliction—that we now ask the attention of the reader.

| SCRIPTURE TESTIMONY |
| :---: |
| *Enter into the joys and* |
| *sorrows of one another* |
| ROMANS 12:15 |

In this particular, Billy Bray may
be almost said to have had a chiv-
alrous sense of duty and honour.
Often dependent himself on the
charity of others—for which he was
truly grateful, but not servile or obsequious—he gladly shared with persons
poorer than himself what little he possessed. He could not keep two hats,
one of his friends says, two days, if he knew of a brother in Christ in want
of one. None enjoyed song and prayer and meditation and worship more
than he; but he never once forgot, in the fulness of his joy, that the naked
had to be clothed, and the hungry to be fed. He did not offer unto the
Lord his God that which cost him nothing. He not only poured out all
his heart in devotion to his Saviour, but of his "substance" he willingly
took for the Lord's work. We sometimes get prayer instead of labour, or
labour instead of prayer; beneficence instead of devotion, or devotion
instead of beneficence. Billy Bray had not so learned Christ. His religion
was not one-sided, but fully developed in every direction. It was bright
in its Godward aspects, but it also beamed on men with tenderness, and
offered them its gifts of love and service. When he had exhausted his own
little store in ministering unto the wants of the poor, he sought for them
help from others. In one instance of this kind, a gentleman, to whom he
applied, gave him a sovereign for some poor persons, and his lady also
gave him some clothes for them. After he had had tea, he said he must
pray before he left the house, for he felt it as much his duty to pray in a
rich man's house as in a poor man's. The gentleman and lady, with some
of their servants, knelt together at His footstool who is "King of kings,
and Lord of lords," while Billy poured out all his heart, for he had sweet
access to the throne of grace. Some Quaker friends, whose kindness to
Billy all through life was very marked, were also appealed to and with the
three pounds he collected he bought food and clothing for the family of
a "quiet, thrifty, honest man,"—and what was a great recommendation
to Billy, one who neither drank nor smoked, —paid their quarter's rent,

filled the collage with sunshine and gladness, and received himself the blessing of those that were ready to perish.

Visits to such devoted Christians as *Peggy Mitchell*, the best scholar in Gwennap parish, because she could read her "title clear to mansions in the skies," were their own exceeding great reward, and it was passing strange to Billy that the duty of visiting the sick should be so much neglected. But the unconverted he sought out as well, and his message of mercy in many a sick chamber God signally blessed. Sometimes young persons of good position accompanied him to the house of mourning, who were both greatly blessed, and made a blessing. These, notwithstanding earthly distinctions and differences, were his brethren and sisters in Christ Jesus, and therefore greatly beloved for His sake. As he had great tact and discretion, besides unfailing cheerfulness, his visits were by many eagerly sought and highly prized. To one who had been a great sufferer for many years, he said, "The pain of yesterday and last night you will never feel any more. You are as well off as the queen so far as *yesterday* is concerned. With the queen yesterday is gone, and so is it with you;" or as another sufferer said to him, she could praise God, "for every pain is a pain the less." Another person whom he visited the same day, an aged Christian eighty years old, —he tells us knew quite as much about the dear Lord as he could tell her. She loved the Lord so much that she did not know a name *good enough* by which to call Him. "Every word she spoke was sweet to my soul," Billy said. And why? he inquires. Because she was filled, as were Barnabas and Stephen, with the Holy Ghost. *"And Satan can do nothing by 'they' who are filled with the Holy Ghost."* Another dear Christian, of five and forty years standing, seen, too, the same day, was one after his own heart, because the Lord had converted her *"in and out"* in allusion to the excessive "outward adorning" of some, which Billy strongly condemned.

(Sometimes in his public addresses, in allusion to the artificial flowers with which so many "women professing godliness" adorn themselves, he would say, "I wouldn't mind your having a waggon-load of them on your heads, if that would do you any good; but you know it wouldn't, and all persons know *that flowers only grow in soft places.*" And many persons can testify that men who made themselves ridiculous by their conceited airs and fine dress did not escape his well-merited and striking rebukes. The nice-ly-feathered arrow from his well-strung bow has often gone much below the surface. His spirit was always stirred within him when he saw men who spent more time in "oiling their cobs," or "twirling their whiskers," than in prayer or the reading of the Bible. Pity that so many should be found to labour in trying to "destroy the fence that separates the Church from the world," and to make by-standers believe that they are more concerned to exhibit the graces of their persons than they are to display the beauties of holiness, or the glories of their Divine Redeemer).

About the same time he found out another person, *whose class-leader had not been to see her but once for a whole year*, and he marvelled not that many became therefore indifferent to heavenly things. He was not sanguine about every case. He saw a person who had been very wicked, and was told that he had been seeking the Lord a long time. He hoped he had; but he added, "It is dangerous to put off our soul's salvation until we art on our death-bed; *for where there is one who gets the prize, there are ten who lose it, and the same old devil that got at them down-stairs will get at them when they are in their beds.*" An old woman who, with a crippled daughter lived in one little dirty down-stairs room, had a word of encouragement. She had had many trials, but she was very hopeful and trusting. The storm had stripped her little cot of its roof, but the Lord had in mercy spared both her and her daughter. Billy said to her, "Heaven will be a 'pretty' place for you when you get there. You will be able to say, 'What a glorious place I am in now? I am not now down in the house with the roof blown away; I am not down now in a dirty little room, with little meat and clothes; —oh, what a mighty change is this! What a glorious place is heaven!'" and he adds, "I believe if any will know the joy of heaven in its higher state, it will be those who have suffered most down here."

I went with Billy one day to visit a preacher, who while he was conversing and praying with him became remarkably happy. Presently the sick man expressed a hope that the Lord would take him to heaven, there and then, as he felt quite ready for the change, and he should not then grieve his best Friend again by carelessness or unbelief. His wife, who was standing by the side of the bed, turned away, her eyes filled with tears. To her

Billy immediately turned and said, "So you would not like to have your husband promoted, then?" And then he took up his parable. "Don't you think that your eye ought to be as much upon the Lord Jesus Christ, as the eye of a worldly woman is upon the Queen? Now if the Queen were to send for the brother, or son, or husband of any such woman, would not she say, 'I am sorry to part with him, but it may be the making of him, I must let him go. *It is the Queen who has sent for him.*' And yet you know," he continued, "that it might be a great expense to prepare him to go; or the Queen might soon die, or he offend her, and then he would be as bad off as ever. But the Lord Jesus Christ is at the expense of the '*fit out,*' He provides the robe in which your husband will be clothed, the crown that he will wear, the palm that he will wave; the Lord Jesus Christ will never die, and your husband wants to go because he knows he shall never offend Him again: *now ought you not to be willing?*" The distressed wife, who was now smiling through her tears, said she was willing, but she did not want to lose him just yet. "And do you think," said Billy, "that you will ever be willing. If my 'Joey' lives, and if I am to wait until she is willing for me to go to heaven, I shall never get there. The fact is, the Lord has a right to take your husband, or me, or any of His children whenever He pleases, *and if I were the Lord I would too, and not ask anybody.*"

I well remember having a visit from Billy when, to all appearances, I was on the borders of the grave, and too weak to join in conversation, or to hear other persons talk much. But Billy intermingled, in a very striking manner, prayer and conversation, addressing earnest exhortations to me, with passionate entreaties to Jehovah. He hoped, he believed, he felt sure that the Lord would raise me up; then I was exhorted to be faithful, to make full proof of my ministry, to bear a good testimony for Christ always; and then he burst out into a glowing description of the honours and dignities which in that case should be my reward, —I was to have a robe, a palm, a throne, a kingdom, a crown, a crown of glory, a crown of life, a crown of righteousness, —and he interposed the remark—I hardly knew whether it was in tended for God or myself, but it nearly convulsed me with laughter—"And I'll wage it will be a fine and pretty one"

There is no doubt about the brightness of Billy's crown, or the fulness of his reward, for in various ways he turned "many to righteousness," and he shall therefore shine forth "like the sun in the kingdom of our Father," or as the "stars for ever and ever."

How just and beautiful are the following remarks respecting Billy's piety, with which we may fitly close this chapter: —"Religion to him was not a duty to be done—not a privilege to be enjoyed in leisure hours—not a benefit-club, a comfortable provision for 'rainy days;' —it was a life. Never left behind, never put off with the Sunday clothes, never hidden before great or low, good or bad—but in him, flowing through him, speaking in every word, felt in every action, seen in every look— deep, true, abiding religion was with him altogether a life. Dead indeed unto sin, he was now living unto God through Jesus Christ.

"Billy had 'lighted his candle,' and resolved that it should give light to all that were in the house. His religion was not a safety-lamp, laid by till he should be going down into the dark valley—nor like the chapel gaslight, that burned only on Sundays and at the week-evening services. Once lighted, it was put into perhaps a commonplace sort of a candlestick, but all at home could see by it. And as the world about him was 'a dark world,' he thrust his candle into a lantern and took it forth wherever he went, and guided not a few from 'horrible pits' that threatened them into the way of salvation. One thing about this lighted candle Billy never forgot—that it burned none the worse for every candle *that was lighted from it.*"

# CHAPTER VII.

## SABBATH KEEPING.

*"If thou turn away thy foot from the Sabbath, from doing thy pleasure on my holy day; and call the Sabbath a delight, the holy of the Lord, honourable; and shalt honour Him, not doing thine own ways, nor finding thine own pleasure, nor speaking thine own words: then shalt thou delight thyself in the Lord; and I will cause thee to ride upon the high places of the earth, and feed thee with the heritage of Jacob thy father; for the mouth of the Lord has spoken it." — Isaiah 58:13, 14.*

ONE OF the most marked features of Billy's character was his love and reverence for the Sabbath. It was to him a day "most calm, most bright," the "pearl of days" in his estimation, to both rich and poor, to the poor especially. If the working men of England only prize the Sabbath as they should, for it comes to them freighted with health, and blessing, and comfort, they will never permit it to be wrested from their grasp under any pretence whatever. An attempt made soon after his conversion to rob Billy of this boon signally failed. He showed on that occasion great wisdom and boldness. Before his conversion he had spent his Sabbaths in idleness and sin, afterwards they were sanctified unto the Lord.

One of the levels of the mine in which he worked filled with water every twelve hours, which was then drawn to the surface. When it came

to Billy's turn one Sunday to go to the mine to draw up the water, he
was at Hicks Mill Chapel. The Lord said to him, "Stay here, and worship
me this day." Billy had no doubt that the Lord did thus speak, or that it
was his duty to obey. "I will, Lord," was his answer, and he left the water
to find its way to the bottom of the shaft, in the full belief that no harm
would come of it. On the Monday morning he went to the mine at six
o'clock, for he could not safely leave the water to take care of itself on the
Monday, though he could do so with great confidence on the Sunday. The
"captain" interrogated him as to his absence, and Billy frankly told him
"it was the Lord's will that he should not work on Sundays." "I'll Lord's
will thee!" the "captain" angrily said; "thou shalt not work here any more."
Billy was unmoved, "for I felt," he said, "that I had the Lord of rocks and
hills for my Friend, and I did not care who was against me." But when
his comrade told him that he was turned away too, he quickly said, "You
must not be turned away on my account; it was not your fault, and I'll
go to the 'captain' and tell him so." At this interview, the "captain" told
Billy he must give up that foolish notion about not working on Sundays,
for men in a mine must work Sundays. Billy replied, "For the wickedness
of the wicked the land mourneth; and I have a new Master now, and He
tells me I must not work on the Sabbath-day, but keep it holy; and I shall
do as He tells me." The clerk in the countinghouse said, if he felt like
William Bray, he wouldn't work on Sundays either. The "captain" then
said he might go to work if he would, and Billy's full cup ran over when
he gave him such work to do as left him at liberty to go to the meetings
every night of the week as well as Sundays.

About the same time a revival began at Twelveheads Chapel, and believing it was the Lord's will he left his barrow and the ash-heap (the new
work to which he had been appointed), and away to the chapel. "I was
much wanted," he tells us, "for the old professors were very dead at that
time, would come into the chapel with their hats under their arm, and
look very black at us. But the Lord was with us, and soon tore a hole in
Satan's kingdom. We had, I think, nearly a hundred converted in one
week, the first week I ever worked all the time for the Lord in His house."
On the Friday of that blessed week, it was "taking-on" day at the mine.

He thought at first he would go, but his second thought was, "No, I will stay here this week, and work for the Lord." "That same night," his account continues, "two men came to the chapel to me, called me out, and said I was appointed to work with them in 'chapel's shaft,' for Captain Hosken, who a little before had turned me away, had told them to take me with them. So I stayed that week and worked for the Lord; and on Monday morning I went to see the place that the Lord had got for me. At the place I had been turned away from I got only £2 a month; and in this new place I had £5 a month or more;[1] and had not to work so hard by a great deal. And so the Lord cleared my way for ever from working Sundays. I did not lose by serving the Lord, but got £3 a month more than I got before; and did the will of the Lord, *which is better than all the money in the world.*" And whatever ridicule may be poured upon his statements that he heard the voice of God forbidding him to do this, and directing him to do that, or upon his belief that God would not suffer any harm to be done by the water on the Sunday, surely all must admire his fidelity to his conscience and his God, and his courage in acting up to his convictions of truth and duty, whatever the result might be to himself. And, after all, what are the incidents just related but illustrations of the Scripture, "Them that honour me, I will honour." And if men only simply and honestly believed what God has promised, such examples would be of daily occurrence, for "none ever trusted in Him, and was confounded."

Much more of the same kind might be added. In the freshness of his first love, Billy had asked on a Sunday morning, "What can I do to be more acceptable in the sight of the Lord than I have already done?"

| SCRIPTURE TESTIMONY |
|---|
| *The fulness of God's joy comes through obedience* |
| JOHN 15:11 · GALATIANS 5:22 · PHILIPPIANS 4:4 · HEBREWS 12:2 |

---

1   I am not quite sure, as the different accounts furnished by Billy's friends are not quite clear and consistent, but it is probable that his being put to work in this particular spot was intended as a punishment, perhaps his "captain" had not quite overcome his chagrin at Billy's refusal to work on a Sunday. He and his comrades could not make much progress, a great part of their time being employed in drawing off the water. In the ear of the Most High he poured his complaints. Almost immediately on resuming his work they heard a sort of gurgling with the water below, and in a little time they had a dry place to work in, and the result was in every respect satisfactory.

The answer he received was, "Fast this day for the Lord's sake." "I will, Lord," was his prompt answer. He did not take any food until eight o'clock at night; and that was the best day he had had for twenty-nine years. Henceforth he took no food from Saturday night until four or five o'clock on Sunday afternoons. His neighbours were afraid that he would starve himself, and a good man, Richard Verran by name, kindly said to him, "The devil is trying to starve thee, for he knows what great things the Lord has done for thee." Billy's answer was, "Richard, the devil shall not starve me, for I can soon know by asking the Lord, who will tell me whether I am right or no." On the next Sunday morning he knelt on a stool and said, "Lord, Thou knowest what the people are saying, that I shall starve myself if I fast; now, my dear Lord, if I must not fast make me happier than I have been." But he did not feel happier. Then he said, "Lord, must I fast?" and he says, "The power of God came down upon me, so that I fell off the stool; and I was convinced that it was the will of the Lord that I should fast." What the people said had no effect upon him now; and truly, as he declares, "If the members of the churches would *mortify* the flesh more, and not *gratify* it, they would be much happier than they are." To his friends who pressed him to eat he would say, "On the Sunday I get my breakfast and dinner from the King's table, two good meals too, and I would not exchange this food from heaven for the richest dinner on the earth." However long might be the journey he had to take, he never altered his practice. And on the Sunday, incessantly occupied as he was, singing, praying, exhorting, in addition to his bodily exertions, for he would be jumping and dancing almost every moment when not otherwise engaged, he never seemed to want food, and I never saw him appear either dull or fatigued. To him the promise seemed literally fulfilled—"They that wait upon the Lord shall renew their strength; they shall mount up with wings as eagles; *they shall run and not be weary; and they shall walk and not faint.*" After rather a long journey one Sabbath to his appointments, when he was got an old man, a good friend on his return said to him, "Poor old man, come, are you?" Billy leaped on the floor, and said, "Don't call me an old man, for I am like a boy. I could go the same journey again, for I'm not one bit weary." At another time, after a very hard day's work he said to a friend, "How strong I am! I am as strong as a lion. I could run up to St Austell (a distance of twenty miles or so), I am so strong."

After he started one Sabbath morning to take his appointments at Mevagissey, he was then living at Tywardreath Highway, he felt very unwell, but to the suggestion, of the enemy as he supposed, that he had better return, he said, "No, I won't. The dear Lord can help me, and I shall go." The pain soon ceased, and if there was any remaining weakness, when he descended from the pulpit, after the morning service, he shouted and jumped it all away. Mr Wesley's sure remedy for cold and hoarseness, was, we believe, more preaching. A happy meeting seemed to be all that Billy Bray required for either body or soul. On the occasion referred to above, he said, "This is the way to make old people young again. If you will get into the Lord's mill, He will grind you down, and make you come out like new ones." Then, instead of going to dinner, he went to visit the sick, it being his meat and drink to do his heavenly Father's will.

There was, too, a beautiful harmony about Billy's Christian character and consistency. He who will not "rob God" will not defraud

> SCRIPTURE TESTIMONY
>
> *True disciples are known by their fruit*
>
> MATTHEW 7:15-22 · LUKE 6:45

his fellow-men; respect for the fourth commandment is a guarantee that the eighth and every other will be scrupulously observed. I am told it is the habit with dishonest miners when they have a good "take" to hide away, when they have the opportunity, some of the ore, so that they may not appear to have been getting too high wages the next "setting-day," and the hidden treasure is reserved and brought out when they are working in a place where the ore is less plentiful and a larger proportion belongs to the "tributer." Against this practice Billy set his face like a flint. "These men could not enjoy religion," he said, "and act the rogue too. What peace of mind could they have when they came to die." Against all deception, fraud, and oppression, he faithfully witnessed, whoever might be the offender, or whatever his rank and position. He sometimes brought upon himself much opposition and reproach for the time, though he carefully watched his temper, that he might not rebuke his brother in a wrong spirit, and for a suitable opportunity, that it might neither be in vain, nor wound the offender unnecessarily. Some of these parties were high-sounding professors; but he well knew if a good conscience be not maintained, of faith itself persons will soon make shipwreck.

A friend of the writer's, naturally of a rather gloomy turn, had much peace and joy during a long illness that ended in death. Speaking to his widow as to the cause of this, which seemed in one of his temperament somewhat remarkable, she said that her husband gratefully noticed the fact, and next to the hope of salvation which he had through Jesus Christ, he thought that it was because he had *never once knowingly cheated any one of a lump of coal*, his business being that of a coal-merchant. This *practical* Christianity is the want of the world.

# CHAPTER VIII.

## TRIALS AND CONFLICTS.

*"I will put enmity between thee and the woman, and
between thy seed and her seed; it shall bruise thy head
and thou shalt bruise his heel."* — *Genesis 3:15.*

*"Blessed is the man that endureth temptation: for when he
is tried, he shall receive the crown of life, which the Lord
hath promised to them that love Him."* — *James 1:12.*

THE DEVIL knows where I live," was a common saying of Billy's, in
answer to remarks of persons that he knew but little or nothing
of trial and temptation. He was tempted, so he said, to do many
bad things, to swear, to tell lies, &c., and sometimes to end his life by
throwing himself down the "shaft" of a mine. But he told the tempter,
*"old smutty-face"* to do this himself, and see how he would like it, and not,
as too many do, meet Satan more than half-way, go to him, and say, "Hae
na ye some dainty temptation for me to-day now, Daddie Satan? I'm sair
wracked for a coaxing temptation;" but Satan he always resisted, "steadfast
in the faith." Nor was he in the habit of seeking sympathy from others;
but "took joyfully" everything as it came along from the hand of a loving
Father. And more than all, perhaps, he thought "it not *strange* concerning
the fiery trials" which were permitted to come upon him, "as though some

*strange* thing had happened unto him." If temptation were a strange thing, it would be still more strange that Jesus himself "suffered being tempted," that He might be "able to succour them that are tempted." It is marvellous that this power to succour Jesus acquired in the actual conflicts of life.

> **SCRIPTURE TESTIMONY**
>
> *Resist the devil and he will flee from you*
>
> JAMES 4:7

Mr Gilbert says he has heard that in coming home from the mine on one occasion, soon after his conversion, Billy was thinking of several recent accidents, which had proved fatal to some of his acquaintances. On getting near a "shaft" where one or two persons had been killed, Billy's mind became possessed with the thought (he was not altogether free from the superstitions which still linger among persons of his class) that they would appear to him from the invisible world. His fears were greatly excited, and though, like many other troubles, quite imaginary, they were none the less terrible to endure. But he passed the place in safety, and of course saw nothing. On coming near another "shaft," he thought of one or two persons who had been killed there, and he trembled with the thought that he should see them. But he kept on his way, struggling with his emotions as best he could. In passing this second "shaft," he had to cross a bridge. Just as he was about to step on it, it came into his mind that the "devil himself" would meet him on the bridge. This thought thoroughly aroused him, and he exclaimed, "The devil! who is he? what can he do? The devil is a fallen angel! he was turned out of heaven by God! —he is held now in chains! I am Billy Bray! God is my heavenly Father! Why should I fear the devil?" Then strong in the consciousness that God was his defence, he said, as if addressing a visible foe, "Come on, then, thou devil; I fear thee not! Come on, Lucifer, and all demons! Come on, old ones and young ones, black ones and blue ones, fiery and red-hot ones; come on, devil, and all thy ugly hosts!" Then, feeling himself delivered from the fears that had distressed and darkened his mind, he began to sing—

> "Jesus, the name high over all.
> In hell, or earth, or sky:
> Angels and men before it fall,
> And devils fear and fly;"

when he was discovered by some of his neighbours leaping and dancing, and praising the Lord who had again given him the victory!

Not many readers will be able, we suppose, to sympathise with this experience of Billy; but he had trials of another kind which come home

| SCRIPTURE TESTIMONY |
| --- |
| *God will provide for our daily needs* |
| MATTHEW 6:11 |

very closely to the understandings and hearts of many. The Lord was his Shepherd, and so he never came to want. The promise is, "Bread shall be given," and "water is sure; but the Lord's people are often brought into great straits. Many an honest Christian man has found it hard work at times to provide for the daily wants of himself and family. Satan is busy in plying the temptation then that the Lord has forgotten him, and is utterly regardless of his wants. Scanty fare, an empty cupboard, an ill-furnished table, thread-bare clothing, —are these the evidences and proofs of God's favour? And then many careless, godless persons have more than heart can wish. God thus tries the faith of His children, and He delights to honour it. Billy Bray was often thus tried, but God worked out his deliverance. He could wait, or work, or suffer, even die, but he could not sin, nor doubt his best Friend. He came home one "pay-day" from the mine without any money. It was a great trial to him, but he bore it meekly. His wife reproached him with being the cause of their poverty and trials, but he said to her, "The Lord will provide," and just then a person, who had heard of his circumstances, came into the house with a basket of provisions containing all that he and his needed. He might well sing, as we are told he did: —

"Not fearing or doubting,
With Christ on my side,
I hope to die shouting,
The Lord will provide."

When he took some of the money that he had so hardly earned, to pay for something wanted for the chapels which he did so much to build, his wife declared, "We shall be brought to the Union, if you go on in this way." "Never mind, my dear Joey, the Lord will provide;" and so He did always, often marvellously. Here is one incident from his own lips.

"At one time I had been at work the whole of the month, but had no wages to take up when pay-day came; and as we had no bread in the house, 'Joey' advised me to go up and ask the 'captain' to lend me a few shillings, which I did, and he let me have ten shillings. On my way home I called to see a family, and found they were worse off than myself; for though we had no bread, we had bacon and potatoes, but they had neither. So I gave them five shillings, and went towards home. Then I called on another family, and found them, if possible, in greater distress than the former. I thought I could not give them less than I had given the others; so I gave them the other five shillings, and went home. And Joey said—

"'Well, William, have you seen the captain?'

"'Yes.'

"'Did you ask him for any money?'

"'Yes; he let me have ten shillings.'

"'Where is it?'

"'I have given it away.'

"'I never saw the fellow to you in my life. You are enough to try any one.'

"'The Lord isn't going to stay in my debt very long,' and I then went out. For two or three days after this, Joey was mighty down; but about the middle of the week, when I came home from the mine, Joey was looking mighty smiling, so I thought there was something up. Presently Joey said—

"'Mrs So-and-so has been here to-day.'

"'Oh!'

"'And she gave me a sovereign.'

"'There, I told you the Lord wasn't going to stay in my debt very long; there's the ten shillings, and ten shillings interest.'"

Coming home one Sunday evening from his appointment through a dirty road, Billy stuck in the mud, and in extricating one foot, he tore off the sole of his shoe. Holding it up, now almost useless, he said, "Here, Father, thou knowest that I have worn out these shoes in Thy cause, and I have no money to buy new ones; help me." The Lord heard him in this time of need, and sent speedy relief. A friend the next week said he wanted Billy to accompany him to Truro; and on their arrival he took him first to a shoe shop, and bought for him a pair of shoes, and then to other shops to get some needed articles of clothing.

Billy was very poor when he was converted (a working man who is a drunkard must be very poor); a low-priced fustian jacket was his best, and he said that was better than he deserved; but false shame did not stop him from going out on the Sunday to warn his fellow-men to "flee from the wrath to come." At the request of a servant girl, an unknown Quaker friend gave him a coat and waistcoat, "which suited me," he said, "as if they were made for me; and they served me for years." This reminds me of one of his facetious remarks on a similar occasion. A good friend said to him, "The Lord has told me to give you a coat and waistcoat, but I do not know whether they will fit you." "If the Lord told you to give them to me, they will fit me all right, *for He knows my size exactly.*" It is right to state it was Billy's opinion that almost all the garments which he had given to him fitted him so well because "he and fashion had once quarrelled," and the breach had never been made up.

Billy's deep poverty was shared by many of his fellow-Christians, preachers and others, and his kind Quaker friends showed also no little kindness to them. When the Bible Christian missionaries went out first,

> SCRIPTURE TESTIMONY
>
> *The heart of the believer, like Jesus, is full of compassion*
>
> MATTHEW 9:36-38 · GALATIANS 6:2 · EPHESIANS 4:32 · COLOSSIANS 3:12

their salary was very small, and sometimes they had to get meat and clothes where they could. "The love of Christ constrained them," and many of them cheerfully endured hardness for His sake. Billy relates this circumstance:—

"One of our preachers was called to preach to a very wicked people, and the Lord made him a great blessing to them. He has told me that, after he has done preaching at night, he has had no place to lodge and nothing to eat. He said that he had slept out in a cold, frosty night, and when he awoke in the morning he found it very hard work to get any heat in himself. The devil tempted him that his case was a bad one, for he had neither food nor lodgings, and his clothes were very poor. He had no friends; and all the people that were pious met in other societies. A member of another society said to him one day, 'You are fine fellows for beating the bushes, but we get the birds.' The missionary then said to him, 'The Day of Judgment is coming, and then every bird-cage door will be thrown open, and every bird will fly to its own cage; and then those will look foolish enough who have got only empty cages in their hand.' This good man suffered hunger and thirst and poverty to do the Lord's will; and the devil was very busy in showing him that the Lord was a hard Master, and so tried to put him out of the way. But he could not, for the dear brother was like St Paul, and could say, 'None of these things move me.' When his clothes got poor, the devil would say, 'See how the Lord is serving thee, for thy clothes is just done, and what wilt thou do then.' But he trusted in the Lord, and the Lord opened the heart of a Quaker friend, who asked him one day, 'Is that all the clothes thou hast got?' And he said 'Yes.' Then the friend said, 'Come to my house, and I will give thee some clothes.' The Lord also opened the heart of another friend, who sent him some money. Then the missionary said, 'Now, devil, I will chase thee all over this mission on penny loaves and water.' So you see that this man loved souls; and he was made a great blessing in the neighbourhood, which had been a wretched one. And the dear Lord will reward the friends who helped him, for He has said, "Inasmuch as ye have done it to one of the least of these my little ones, ye have done it unto me.'"

It was Billy's belief that the Lord "opened" the hearts of his friends to help him whenever he needed it, and "shut" them up when help was no longer required.

Billy had other trials in his family besides those of which we have spoken. He had two sisters, and one of them, who was out of her mind, was very trying. She was sometimes so cross, that she exercised Billy's faith and patience more than a little. But he had one unfailing resort in trouble. "I cried to the Lord, and He heard me, for He made me so happy that I could not hold it in; I had a joy unspeakable and full of glory; I had good measure, pressed down, and running over. *Now what was that trial compared with the blessing I received?* I was so happy that I felt none of these things could move me. I could say, 'I long to be with Christ now. My dear Lord, let me die, and take me to heaven.' I felt so much of the Divine glory that I longed to be there. I cannot tell what I felt." Did he not know what the Saviour meant when He said, "In the world ye shall have tribulation; *but be of good cheer*, I have overcome the world."

And yet one other kind of trial we must mention. During his wife's long illness, which ended in death, he "had many blessed seasons while praying with her, and promises from the dear Lord." At one time the words were so deeply impressed on his mind, "She is mine for ever," that tears came into his eyes. At another time he was greatly comforted by the conviction, inwrought into his heart by the power of the Holy Ghost, that he himself, his wife and family, should be saved. Therefore he said, "I had no reason to doubt of my wife's going to heaven; nevertheless the devil often tempted me that, because I was not home with her when she died, it was not well with her. But the devil could not make me believe it. Since the dear Lord has settled the matter, *the old king of the blacks* does not tempt me that she is not in heaven. When the dear Lord speaks to His children's hearts, He speaks the truth; He is a God of truth, and all who love Him are children of the truth." Thus in all these things was Billy more than a conqueror through Him that loved him.

We may give two or three incidents, as they show not only the eccentricity, but also the force of his genius. He thus repelled the tempter, when he said to him, "I'll have thee down to hell after all." "Hast thee got a little 'lew' place for me in hell where I could sing thee a song? *Thee cus'n't burn me devil. There's no grease in me;*" or, "What an ould (old) fool thee art now; I have been battling with thee for twenty-eight years,[1] and I have always beat thee, and I always shall." But the devil said again, "Well, I'll have thee down to hell after all." But Billy said to him, "I'd as soon go to hell with thee as not. For I'd bring Jesus Christ with me, and shout and sing, and praise the Lord, for that's a sound thee hasn't heard for two seven years, and I know thee wost-en (would not) like that."[2] If the temptation

---

1    This was spoken at the opening of Penhallow Chapel, Truro Circuit
2    Billy's daring faith reminds us of the old Scottish believer of whom Dr Brown speaks in his *Horæ Subsecivæ*. To her pastor, who asked, "Janet, what would you say if, after all He has done for you, God should let you drop into hell?""E'en's [even as]

was that he was a fool to go and preach, as he would never get anything for it, the answer was, "Not so big a fool as thee art, for once thee was in a good situation, and did not know how to keep it."

His own graphic account[1] of how he "beat the devil" when his crop of potatoes failed, is so good, that we gratefully insert it here: —

"Friends, last week I was a-diggin' up my'taturs. It was a wisht poor yield, sure'nough; there was hardly a sound one in the whole lot. An' while I was a-diggin' the devil come to me, and he says, 'Billy, do you think your Father do love you?' 'I should reckon He do,' I says. 'Well, I don't,' says the ould tempter in a minute. If I'd thought about it I shouldn't ha' listened to'en, for his'pinions ben't worth the leastest bit o' notice. 'I don't,' says he, 'and I tell'ee what for: if your Father loved you, Billy Bray, He'd give you a pretty yield o''taturs; so much as ever you do want, and ever so many of'em, and every one of'em as big as your fist. For it ben't no trouble to your Father to do anything; and He could just as easy give you plenty as not, an' if He loved you, He would, too.' Of course, I wasn't goin' to let he talk o' my Father like that, so I turned round'pon'en. ' Pray, sir,' says I, 'who may you happen to be, cornin' to me a-talkin' like this here? If I ben't mistaken, I know you, sir, and my Father, too. And to think o' you cornin' a-sayin' He don't love me! Why, I've got your written character home to my house; and it do say, sir, that you be a liar from the beginnin'! An' I'm sorry to add, that I used to have a personal acquaintance with you some years since, and I served you faithful as ever any poor wretch could: and all you gave me was nothing but rags to my back, and a wretched home, and an achin' head, an' no'taturs, and the fear o' hell-fire to finish up with. And here's my dear Father in heaven. I have been a poor servant of His, off and on, for thirty years. An' He's given me a clean heart, an' a soul full o' joy, an' a lovely suit o' white as'll never wear out; and He says that He'll make a king o' me before He've done, an' that He'll take me home to His palace to reign with Him for ever and ever. An' now you come up here a-talkin' like that.' Bless'e, my dear friends, he went off in a minute, like as if he'd been shot —*I do wish he had—and he never had the manners to say Good*

---

He likes," answered Janet: "if He does, He'll lose mair than I do." Surely that was the sublimity of faith in Him whose word cannot be broken.

1    From "Daniel Quorm, and his Religious Notions."

*mornin'*. "Godliness is profitable unto all things, having the promise of the life which now is, as well as that which is to come; but all true Christians love God for what He is, and not for profit or reward; and they love holiness, not only because it is happiness, but because it is His image who is to them "the fairest among ten thousand, and the altogether lovely." It is a miserable, shallow philosophy to suppose that the Lord rewards those who are poor in spirit, and pure in heart, and patient under suffering, with mere earthly good, or that their trust, and love, and devotion, and service, can be alienated by any sorrows and evils He permits to come upon them.

In resisting temptation, Billy knew the special value of the *shield of faith*, without which any Christian's armour is incomplete. On one occasion, in his capacity as captain-dresser, he engaged to dress a quantity of ore, and had to employ a number of young persons. But the general opinion was, that the lot was all but worthless, and for a time it was a great trial to Billy as there would be nothing for him, and worse still, nothing for those under him. "Why, the people will say, there's that ould (old) Billy Bray, an ould Bryanite, an ould rogue, he hath cheated the boys and maidens of their wages. A pretty Christian he!" But Billy wrestled and laboured in prayer, until he got the assurance that the Lord was on his way (Daniel 10:9). "I will bring thee through," the Lord said to him one day while he was praying; to which gracious word he at once answered, "I believe it, Lord, I know Thee wost( Thou wilt); praise the Lord, amen, glory. I don't care now what the devil says. If Thou tell me that Thou wilt bring me through, I believe Thou wilt." And his foot once placed upon the rock, he was not to be moved. The struggle was again and again renewed, but to all suggestions, from whatever quarter they came, his answer was, "I don't care whether the stuff is worth anything or not. The Lord hath told me He will bring me through, and I believe Him." And did the Lord disappoint His servant? or leave "him at last in trouble to sink?" No, no! On the "sampling" day the "stuff" was found to be more valuable than any person expected, enabling Billy to pay the boys and girls their wages, his own, and then have left for himself.

His own experience taught him the only method, and his occupation as a miner the particular illustration, by which he could inspire his fellow-Christians with steadfastness and courage in the midst of trials. "The best way to serve the devil," he would say, "is to win'en (wind him) up at the capstan. Throw the rope round'en," he continued, "and turn away until you get'en up close to the axle, and when he cries 'strick' (strike), you must'en let go at all, but hold'en fast. If you get'en up tight to the axle, and keep'en there, he'll never be able to harm'e (hurt you): all he will be able to do, will be to grizzle at'e (snarl at you)." It was evident that Billy had got the arch-foe tight at the capstan.

Who can read this account of Billy's temptations without being reminded of Jehovah's declaration to the serpent, "I will put enmity between thee and the woman, and between thy seed and her seed;" and the remainder of that storm of wrath which the devil poured on the head of our blessed Redeemer, he has reserved for His followers, but with the same result in many cases, thank God, as in the case of Jesus himself. Impotent is Satan's fury if we take the whole armour of God.

Billy knew, too, how to fight the devil and his agents with their own weapons. Returning late from a revival meeting, on a dark night, in a lonely road, "certain lewd fellows of the baser sort," tried to frighten him by making all sorts of unearthly sounds; but he went singing on his way. At last one of them said, in the most terrible tones, "But I'm the devil up here in the hedge, Billy Bray." "Bless the Lord! bless the Lord!" said Billy, "*I did not know thee 'wost' so far away as that.'* To use Billy's own expression, "What could the devil do with such as he?"

At a friend's house in Truro, the mistress read the account of the temptation of our Lord at family prayer. Billy listened quietly till the verse was read in which Satan promises the Saviour all the kingdoms of the world, and the glory of them, if He would only fall down and worship him, when he started to his feet exclaiming, "The ould vagabond! the ould vagabond! he give away all the kingdoms of the world when he never had an old tatur skin to call his own, the ould vagabond!"

# CHAPTER IX.

## DRINKING AND SMOKING.

*"What! know you not that your body is the temple of the Holy Ghost*
*which is in you, which ye have of God, and ye are not your own!*
*For ye are bought with a price: therefore glorify God in your body,*
*and in you spirit, which are God's." — I Corinthians 6:20.*

ANY LIFE of Billy Bray would be considered by all who knew him as incomplete that did not refer to his strong detestation of the pernicious habits of taking intoxicating drinks, and of smoking. He bore a lifelong and emphatic testimony against these evils. He had been much debased by drunkenness, and a perfect slave to the pipe. "When I heard," he says, "that Mr Teare was coming to Hicks Mill to lecture on Teetotalism, I thought I would go to hear him, but that I would not sign the pledge; for a little drop, if a man does not take too much, will do him good. As I listened to what Mr Teare had to say, the darkness was removed from my mind, and I thought I would sign the pledge; and before Mr Teare had finished speaking I shouted out to friend Tregaskis, 'Thomas, put down my name!'" and from that hour he was not only a staunch teetotaler, but also one of the most earnest and successful advocates of the great and holy cause of temperance. That so many persons have been saved from sin and shame by the safeguard of teetotalism ought to be a sufficient reason for all good people to render it their support. Billy used to say, so Mr

Ashworth tells us, "'If Satan ever catches me, it will be with the ale-pot. Men set lime-sticks to catch birds, and Satan sets wine-bottles and ale-pots to catch fools, but I will not touch a drop, then I shall never get drunk.'

"At one temperance meeting, speaking of moderation, he said, 'Ye might as well hang an old woman's apron in the gap of a potato field to prevent the old sow with young pigs from going in, as expect a drunkard to be cured with moderation. Satan knows that, so he sets the little pot to catch him again.'"

He also fully endorsed the opinion which he had heard expressed, that public-houses were *hell-houses*. He knew one house where *nineteen* men got drunk, and while in a state of intoxication fell into "shafts," and were killed. "*Hell-houses*" he would say, "indeed they are! —for they are places where people are *prepared for hell*, and they *help* people on their way." But with his love of antithesis, and his habitual cheerfulness, even "hell-houses" reminded him of chapels, where people are converted and prepared for heaven, and therefore might properly be called "*heaven-houses*."

But the evils of drinking are so generally admitted, that we need not insist on the importance of Temperance, or attempt to describe the benefits that come, with autumn ripeness and bountifulness, on all persons who embrace and advocate its principles. But the case is different with the growing evil of *smoking*, and Billy's views thereon we cannot lightly pass over without being unfaithful to his memory. He says—

| SCRIPTURE TESTIMONY |
| --- |
| *God using an inner voice* *to communicate* |
| JOHN 14:26 · ACTS 10:19-20 · ACTS 11:12 |

"I had been a smoker as well as a drunkard, and I used to love my tobacco as much as I loved my meat, and I would rather go down into the mine without my dinner than without my pipe. In the days of old the Lord spoke by the mouth of His servants the prophets; now He speaks to us by the Spirit of His Son. I had not only the feeling part of religion, but I could hear the small still voice within speaking to me. When I took the pipe to smoke, it would be applied within, 'It is an idol, a lust, worship the Lord with *clean lips*.' So I felt it was not right to smoke. The Lord also sent a woman to convince me. I was one day in a house, and I took out my pipe to light it at the fire, and Mary Hawke—for that was the woman's name—said, 'Do you not feel it is wrong to smoke?' I said I felt something inside telling me it is an idol, a lust; and she said that was the Lord. Then I said, 'Now I must give it up, for the Lord is telling me of it inside, and the woman outside; so the tobacco must go, love it as I may.' There and then I took the tobacco out of my pocket, and threw it into the fire, and put the pipe under my foot, 'ashes to ashes, dust to dust.' And I have not smoked since. I found it hard to break off old habits; but I cried to the Lord for help, and He gave me strength, for He has said, 'Call upon me in the day of trouble, and I will deliver thee.' The day after I gave up smoking I had the toothache so bad I did not know what to do. I thought this was owing to giving up the pipe, but I said I would never smoke again if I lost every tooth in my head. I said, 'Lord, Thou hast told us, "My yoke is easy, and my burden is light,"' and when I said that all the pain left me. Sometimes the thought of the pipe would come back to me very strong; but the Lord strengthened me against the habit; and, bless His name, I have not smoked since."

Mr Maynard says that, after Billy had given up smoking, he thought he would chew a little; but he conquered this dirty habit too. "On one occasion," he says, "when at a prayer-meeting at Hicks Mill, I heard the Lord say to me, 'Worship me with clean lips.' So when we got up from our knees, I took the quid (and when speaking of it he would suit the action to the word) out of my mouth, and 'whipp'd en' (threw it) under the form. But when we got on our knees again, I put another 'quid' into my mouth. Then the Lord said to me again, 'Worship me with clean lips.' So I took the 'quid' out of my mouth, and 'whipp'd en' under the form again, and said, 'Yes, Lord, I will.' From that time I gave up chewing as well as smoking, and have been a free man."

Smoking and chewing are expensive and wasteful habits, and this view of the matter is worthy of consideration by working-men who find it difficult to live honestly in the world, and especially by Christian working-men who find it still more difficult to render any but the most trifling pecuniary aid to the cause which they have espoused. More than twenty years after Billy had abandoned smoking, he said, "God has just given me enough money to pay my way through life, and nothing for the pipe. If I had spent only sixpence a week or the pipe I should have been at this time about thirty pounds in debt." A thought surely worthy of the attention of those who indulge in any useless habit at the expense of others and to their own injury.

It was especially a gratification to Billy if he could persuade young men to imitate his example.[1]

He would tell them that the pipe "was no help to them in the way to heaven, but an enemy to body and mind and pocket. When the good Spirit suggests to the mind of a good man to read a chapter in the Bible, the evil spirit which is after the flesh will say, 'I would have a pull at the pipe first;' and by the time he has lit his pipe and smoked, something comes along for him to do, and he does not read at all for that time. When it comes into his mind to pray, it is said, 'I would have a pipe first,' and by the time the pipe is done, something comes in his way that calls him off; and there is no praying for that time. The pipe has robbed the Christian of hundreds of chapters and prayers, besides proving injurious in point of health and wealth.

But persons say, "It is their right, and they will not give it up." But Billy would say they must give up every idol for the Lord's sake, who gave His last drop of blood for them. Once while he was speaking warmly on this subject, a gentleman said he was speaking what was not right. Billy said, "Drink and smoke, is that right? It must be 'drink and smoke,' or 'not drink and smoke.'" The gentleman said no more, and an old man said, "Billy

---

1    "After fifty years of most extensive and varied practice in my profession, I have come to the decision that smoking is a main cause of ruining our young men, pauperising the working-men, and rendering comparatively useless the best efforts of ministers of religion."—*John Higginbottom, Esq., M. R. C. S.*
"The first cigar that a young man puts into his mouth is often his first step in a career of vice."—*John Angell James.*
"Smoking," a clergyman says, "is Satan's seed-basket, with which he beguiles unwary souls."
Mr Scott, the Chamberlain of the City of London, remarks, "The apprentices of the City who violate the covenants of their indentures are amenable to my Court; and my first inquiry invariably is, Does the boy drink? and as invariably the answer is, No. Does he smoke? and in nearly every instance the reply is, Yes." "Seventeen out of twenty cases of criminal offences in Manchester and Salford gaols," says Mr Thomas Wright, "are in connection with smoking and drinking—the former generally preceding the latter." [These quotations are taken from "The Fascinator; or, The Knight's Legacy," a Prize Essay by Mrs Noel-Thatcher, a book which ought to be extensively circulated.]

Bray is right, for I smoked forty years, and it did me no good, and I have given it up now." But Billy had to confess afterwards that the same old man says Billy is wrong; for he had "turned to his idol again, and was a worse smoker than ever." Some who abandoned the habit soon took it up again, and exposed themselves to Billy's sarcasm, "that a little pipe could beat them." He told a person who said that he was tempted, to "go and tell the Lord about it." The man said, "I do not know whether it is the devil who is tempting me or not, for it is continually coming into my mind to give up the pipe." Billy answered, "I do not think that *that* is the devil. I told him to stop, and not throw away his pipe till we had prayed, and cast lots, and if it came to his lot to throw the pipe away he should. We knelt down, and asked the Lord to show us by the lot what we ought to do; and as it came for him to give up his pipe, he threw it away for the time. After a day or two he said to me, he thought there was some good in the pipe after all. Then I said to him, 'Thee hast cut the head of the beer-quart off, but only chopped the tail of the tobacco-pipe off; thee wilt have it again soon.' And he did, but after a while he gave it up finally."

Billy was particularly hard upon preachers through whose example many, he believed, of the Lord's people were induced to depart from the right way. He considered no favour should be extended to them. He was hardly at liberty to be charitable in the matter, for it was the Lord's work, and soon all would have to answer for their conduct in the judgment; some for continuing to smoke, and others for giving it up, and he felt confident as to what the decision of the Great Judge would be. "If the preachers smoke, I may smoke too," was the argument he felt he could not answer, except by bringing a *charge* against the preachers, which he was most unwilling to do. "*Defile* not yourselves with idols," and "*Mortify* the deeds of the body," were, in Billy's view, such definite commands, that for Christians to smoke seemed to him to be the most glaring inconsistency.

Billy and a preacher of somewhat the same type of character were holding a missionary meeting at F---------. Billy opened the meeting with prayer, and the preacher and others fervently responded to many of his petitions. Observing this, he began to be more minute and pointed in his requests. "O Lord, help the people to give up their idols." The preacher said, "Amen." "May Thy children be saved from the love of the world's fashions." "Amen," again said the preacher. "Help Thy people to give up their ribbons and feathers." "Amen," was still the response of the preacher; and again "Amen" when he added, "And their cups and drinks." "And their pipes and tobacco," but to this there was no "Amen" from the preacher. Billy at once said, "Where's your Amen, Br. B--------? Why don't you say 'Amen' to the pipes as well as the cups? Ah! you won't say 'Amen' to the pipes!" He then proceeded with his prayer. And what would be irreverent in most persons, did not appear so in him. But the preacher afterwards remonstrated with Billy on his impropriety in administering this personal rebuke in public. He justified himself by saying, "You were hearty and loud enough with your 'Amens' for others to give up their idols; but you are not willing to part with your own. Bless the Lor! I have given up *all* for my Saviour."

At one time the same preacher was preaching when Billy Bray was present; warming with his subject, he exclaimed, "If my arms were long enough and strong enough, and God would give me permission, I would take you all and fly right away to heaven with you!" "And I," said Billy Bray, "would be back again in half an hour for another turn."

Persons sometimes are laughed out of idle habits, when serious remonstrance and Scriptural appeals are in vain. Billy frequently said, that if God intended man or woman to take snuff, the nose would have been turned upside down; and that an architect who built a house without a chimney, so that all the smoke came out at the front door, was in his opinion a very poor architect. "And if the Lord intended men to smoke, He certainly would have made a little chimney at the back of the head for the smoke to pass through; but as He has not, I don't think He intended for man to smoke; for surely the Lord could not be a worse architect than man."

# CHAPTER X.

## REBUKE AND EXHORTATION.

*"If thou forbear to deliver them that are drawn unto death, and
those that are ready to be slain; if thou sayest, Behold, we knew it
not; doth not He that pondereth the heart consider it? and He that
keepeth thy soul, doth not He know it? and shall not He render
to every man according to his works?" Proverbs 24:11, 12.*

"BILLY," WRITES a friend, "was so completely absorbed with a desire
to do good—so fired with zeal for the honour of his Divine
Master—so full of pity towards his fellow-men—so saved from
the fear of man which bringeth a snare—and so impressed with an habitual sense of God's presence and favour, that, without regard to position,
or rank, or character, or circumstances, he was ever ready to testify of
the reality and blessedness of religion, or to administer such reproof, or
counsel, or warning as he deemed necessary. At one time he might be seen
in the midst of a group of pleasureseekers, seeking to impress them with
the idea, that real and lasting pleasure was to be had only in religion; at
another time he might be found in the midst of an angry, quarrelsome
party, striving to conciliate by kind entreaties and loving arguments, or
perhaps on his knees, asking God to be merciful, and soften the hearts
of the angry ones, calling them by name; and anon you might have seen
him accosting strangers, whom he met on the roads or in the streets, or

hailing certain persons with whose characters and peculiar tendencies he
appeared quite familiar, and abruptly, some fastidious persons might say,
even rudely, but always cheerfully and lovingly, saying something about
Christ and His salvation."

His wonderful tact and address in speaking to friends and strangers
personally, whether it came by nature or grace, or in part from one and
in part from the other, was certainly one of the most marked features of
his character. And yet he did not belong to that class of men who have
been called "religious *chatterers*." He had "such an insight into people," he
had "such a sense of times and seasons," he had "such a power of putting
the truth in an available form, that men could take it without hesitation,
and digest it, as it were." He seemed to be one of those "unordained men
that are ordained of God from their birth to be teachers in this way." His
heart seemed to take such "hold of persons," as led him to "think about
them, and pray for them, and brood over them" with the tenderest, purest
affection and sympathy. But his talents were multiplied by the wise and
benevolent use he made of them; and to persons who say, "I have not the
power he had; and if I had I should not know how to use it," it may be
said, as has been said in a similar case, "But it does not follow you ought
not to learn; for the *learning* is very essential." The church needs the power
to preach to individuals, and to preach, as did her Divine Lord, her best
sermons, too, on such occasions.

| SCRIPTURE TESTIMONY |
| :---: |
| *The sheep know and hear His voice* |
| JOHN 10:3-4 · JOHN 10:16 |

"Brethren, if a man be overtaken
in a fault, ye which are spiritual
restore such an one in the spirit of
meekness; considering thyself, lest
thou also be tempted." We may best
learn what this means by an example. Billy says, "At the time I was building
Bethel Chapel, I knew a very good man, but who had a very wicked woman
for his wife. She persecuted him in various ways, sometimes by throwing
water in his face. One day she provoked him so much that he swore. He
at once keenly felt that he had grievously sinned. Very earnestly did he
ask the Lord to have mercy on him, Satan busily telling him all the while
that it was no use to pray, for no one would believe in him again. When

I was working about the chapel the Lord spoke to me and said, 'Go up and restore thy brother.' So I threw down the shovel that I was working with, and away I went to his house. When I got there his wife began to curse him, and to tell me what her husband had said. When she had done I told her what the Lord said to the Jews when the woman was taken in adultery, 'He that is without sin among you, let him first cast a stone at her.' I asked the husband to walk out with me. I then said, 'Is not the devil telling you that it is no use to pray, and that nobody will believe in you any more?' 'Yes,' he said. Then I told him that the dear Lord had sent me to him, and that He was on his side, and that I was on his side, and while I was talking to him the dear Lord sent another brother to encourage him. And on the following Sunday the darkness was all dispersed, he regained the blessing he had lost, lived and died trusting in the Saviour, while his wife, continuing to harden her heart, and make the path of her husband rough and difficult, was soon removed by death, to answer, at the judgment-seat of Christ, for all that she had done."

"In meekness instructing those that oppose themselves; if God peradventure will give them repentance to the acknowledging of the truth; and that they may recover themselves out of the snare of the devil, who are taken captive by him at his will." Billy had learnt the meaning of this Scripture also. When he was out one Sunday beating up recruits for the evening service, he met with a man "who used to say that though Jesus was a good man, He had not all power, and that there was no such being as the devil; there was, he said, no other devil than the wickedness that was in man. He was a scholar, and thought to be a very wise man. One day when he was arguing that there was no devil, and that all a man had to mind was his own wicked heart, I asked *him what wickedness it was that went into the swine* and drove them over the cliff? He asked me how it was that the Lord suffered the swine to be driven over the cliff? And I said to him, for two reasons, it seems to me, First, to show the *power* of God; and then to show the envy of the devil, who would *rather go into the swine than nowhere.* Then he said, 'You nearly always beat me.' But since we used to argue like that the Lord has made him a new creature," one of the many whom Billy turned to righteousness.

"When a man's ways please the Lord, He will make even his enemies to be at peace with him." Mr Wooldridge says,

| SCRIPTURE TESTIMONY |
| --- |
| *Love your enemies and do good to them* |
| LUKE 6:32-35 |

"An old gentleman once took great umbrage at Billy's faithful reproofs and lively manner in giving prominence to divine things in everyday life, and at last he became all but inveterate in his hatred to one who strove to acknowledge God in all his ways. But when affliction overtook him, and death and judgment and eternity appeared close at hand, he found that his lamp gave neither light nor warmth. The happy Christian man, the once dreaded enemy, in the same sense as Elijah was the enemy of Ahab, was now sent for, to do for the unhappy man what David did for Saul, play upon his harp, so that the evil spirit of melancholy might depart from him. On Billy's entering the sick chamber, looking around on the costly furniture, he spoke aloud, and yet as if he were speaking to himself, 'Did Jesus Christ ever occupy such a fine place as this? or spend money to gratify fleshly desire and worldly taste?' Then, in a strain of tenderness and pity, he began to commiserate Jesus on His deep poverty while sojourning here below, till the bystanders were annoyed, and the old gentleman flushed with indignation and wrath. But when Billy had, as he thought, probed the wound enough, he applied the healing balm. And while he was praying, a sweet peace stole over the sufferer's mind and greatly comforted his troubled heart. Billy was now asked to stay with the sick man until his departure hence, which was not till two or three weeks afterwards. Billy had some of the sorest conflicts he ever experienced during that time, but in every instance he came off victorious through the blood of the Lamb, was more than a conqueror through Him that loved him. The old gentleman, too, again and again lost his hold of God, but Billy as often rendered the help which the poor man who lay so long at Bethesda's pool so much needed. He kept him whom he had under his care in contact, as it were, with the truth, and the Spirit, and the Saviour, till his mind underwent a complete transformation. At last he could no longer doubt that the day of eternal brightness and joy had dawned, for the 'day-star had arisen in his heart.' The light of the 'city that hath no need of the sun' shone all around, and without a cloud he passed away to his home in the skies. Billy left the house early one summer's morn, with the last practical proof of the old gentleman's gratitude in his pocket, when he met an absent son from a distance on his way to see his father. To his inquiry how he was, Billy joyfully answered, 'Never so well in all his life, for he is just gone off with the beautiful shining ones!'" Shall we be forgiven if we say here that a little boy once said to his mother that he "reckoned there would be a pretty row in heaven when his father and Billy Bray got there;" and at another time that he thought Billy Bray would never get to heaven, "because he would kick the angels so much while they were carrying him up that they wouldn't carry him any further, but let him fall." While the child's fears may excite a smile, we know that Billy's happy spirit, once released from the burden of the flesh, did, as it were, with one bound, enter into the joy of his Lord.

In January 1867, Billy went to Plymouth and Devon-port to hold some meetings for the Primitive Methodists, for he was no bigot, and was willing to serve all to the best of his ability, because he loved all them that loved the Lord Jesus Christ in sincerity. They had *blessed* meetings, rather noisy too. A man reproved Billy in the street for making so much noise. "He spoke very sharp, and said he did not mind who heard him. He was not ashamed to *do* his Master's work out in the street, and I am sure we who love the Lord ought not to be ashamed to praise Him in the chapel. I told the man that I did not fear him, nor his black-faced master; and if I had hearkened to such as he I should have lost my best friend long ago. My best friend is the dear Lord; He has made me *glad*, and no one can make me sad; He makes me *shout*, and there is no one who can make me *doubt*; He it is that makes me *dance and leap*, and there is no one that can keep down my *feet*. I sometimes feel so much of the power of God that, I believe, *if they were to cut off my feet I should heave up the stumps.*"

Billy was emphatically a *happy* Christian; he rejoiced in the Lord always. His friend Mr Haslam interrogated him on one occasion as to the secret of his *constant* happiness, comparing Billy's experience with his own. He was not always, he said, on the Mount; his prospects were sometimes clouded; his fears rather than his faith prevailed at times; he therefore wanted to know how it was that Billy got on so much better than he did. Billy answered that we must become fools for Christ's sake; that Christians, like Mr Haslam, who had so much *'book-larnin'*, were placed at a disadvantage, when compared with some others, having so much to unlearn, *"for some of us, you know,"* Billy naively added, *"are fools to begin with."*

On most occasions, Billy's wit sparkled and flashed without effort apparently on his part; but he knew how to hold it in reserve when persons sought merely to gratify their curiosity, or wished him to display his powers for their amusement. Some such got more than they bargained for. Thus, to a lady who once "interviewed" him for this purpose, he was very silent and reserved. She, hoping to draw him out, said, "You know we must be willing to be fools for Christ's sake." "Must we, ma'am?" was his ready answer; *"then there is a fair of us!"*

Reproached one day by a depraved, dissolute man, as being one of those idle fellows who go about living upon others, and doing nothing whatever, he said, "My Father can keep me a gentleman always if He pleases, without my doing any work at all; but your father"—pointing to his shabby tattered garments—"cannot even keep you in decent clothes with all your hard work." "Answer not a fool according to his folly, lest thou be like unto him. Answer a fool according to his folly, lest he be wise in his own conceit;" *i.e.,* "If fools talk nonsense, do not talk nonsense with them; if fools boast a victory over wisdom, then let wisdom expose their folly."

When some person, on one occasion, asked Billy how the world was getting on now, he answered, "I don't know, for I haven't been there for twelve years."

# CHAPTER XI.

## FULLY RIPE FOR THE GARNER.

*"Thou shalt come to thy grave in a full age, like as a shock
of corn cometh in in his season."* — *Job 5:26.*

HAVING NEARLY filled the space allotted me, I notice in reading
what I have written, that the subjects so run into one another,
that my purpose to keep them separate and distinct has not been
fully accomplished; and that I have dealt with the flowers and fruits, rather
than with the roots and the principles of the Christian life.

There are also some points which in my plan had separate chapters
assigned to them which have hardly been noticed; and Billy's evangelistic
labours was one, in which he succeeded in first winning the *ear*, and then
the *heart*, and thus introducing the gospel into many places; his view of
the sin and danger of worldly conformity was another, under which head
his opposition to holding *bazaars* to raise money for religious purposes,
to *choir* singing in the public worship of God's house, when the singers
are unconverted, and to preachers and members, especially the former,
allowing their *beards* to grow long, according to the prevailing fashion,
might very properly have been discussed. Some will regard this last-named
particular as an indication of essential narrowness of mind. But he was
ready to make excuses for those persons who, he believed, allowed their
beards to grow long for the sake of their health, but he could not tolerate

them for one moment if he believed that persons did so for pride, or love of show and fashion. Perhaps it was a struggle in all cases for him to overcome his prejudices against long beards! Let the reader call it a weakness in him, or what he will, it was with him a matter of conscience, and where one is to be found who is scrupulous to a fault in little matters, a hundred may be found who pay no heed to conscience whatever. In the company of many "long-bearded" men he once said, "If I thought you did it for the sake of Christ I should not care, but I am afraid they are too plenty to be good." One of them said, "They came by nature, I suppose." "True," said Billy, "and do you suppose that heaven ever designed everything should remain in its natural state? Do you prune your fruit-trees, or allow them to grow wild, just as they please? It is only a foolish man that would use such an argument."

It might be thought, too, that a man who had so given himself up to the public, must have *neglected*, in some measure, his own family and friends; but he fully believed in the ancient covenant of Jehovah that he would be the God of the righteous, and to *their seed after them;*[1] and gladly obeyed the command of the Saviour: "Go home to thy friends, and tell them how great things the Lord hath done for thee, and had compassion on thee." Wife, children, brother, mother, uncle, and other relatives, believed because of his word, and had the great reward of faith in the blessing of a joyful experience, already forming quite a large group in the kingdom of eternal glory.

Billy always enforced the principle that the "best" should be given unto the Lord, and not the "blind," the "lame," or the "sick." At one time at a Missionary meeting he seemed quite vexed because there was something said in the report about money received for "rags and bones." And when he rose to address the meeting, he said, "I don't think it is right, supporting the Lord's cause with old rags and bones. The Lord deserves the best, and ought to have the best.[2] However, He is very condescending, for when a person has a little 'chick' that is likely to die, puts it into a stocking, and lays it by the fire, saying, 'If that "chick" lives, I will give it to the Missionaries,'

1   Genesis 17:7.
2   Mr Spurgeon's comment on this is, "Well done, Billy! This is right good, and sound divinity"

it is not long before it says, 'Swee, swee,' let me out, I am better. I knew a woman down at St Just some years ago who had two geese, and though she might have a good flock to begin, she could never rear above two or three. At last she promised the Lord if He would increase her flock she would give every *tenth* goose to the Missionaries. Now I reckon," he continued, "you will say that that woman was a good heart; but I don't think so, for if she gave every *fifth* goose to the Missionaries she would have then more than she had before. However, the Lord took her at her word, and the next year she had *eleven*, and they all lived till they grew up nearly as big as old ones, and then the Lord tried her faith, one of her geese died. And what do you think the devil said? *'That's the Missionary goose!'* That's as the devil would serve the Missionaries; he would give old, dead, stinking geese to them to eat, but what do they want of an old, dead, stinking goose? But she knew 'un,' and she said, 'No, devil, I have ten left now, and the Missionaries shall have one of them.' And the next year she had eleven again. They were out swimming about the pond, with their great long necks and their beautiful white feathers, *they were the most respectablelooking geese I ever saw.*"

As already stated, Billy was a most earnest and successful Missionary advocate, though some of his arguments and illustrations at times were not altogether unobjectionable. I well remember on one occasion his strongly urging the people, both the converted and unconverted, to contribute, those who were converted, out of gratitude, and those who were not, because it might give them greater confidence if they should ever seek mercy and forgiveness at the Lord's hands. An old Independent minister, who had kindly lent his chapel for the meeting, sitting by my side, said to me at once, I suppose you would not like to vouch for the soundness of his theology, and before I had time to answer, Billy was in the midst of an illustration of his meaning that set us all in a roar of laughter. He knew a young man once who had been very wicked, and when convinced of his great sinfulness by the Spirit of God, he despaired for a long time of finding mercy. Billy among others tried to comfort him; but to all they said he only answered, "As I have never done anything for the Lord, *I have not, I really have not got the cheek to ask Him to bestow on me so great a blessing as the forgiveness of my sins."* But the thought, later, that he had once given five shillings to help on the Lord's cause, at a time when help was much needed, greatly encouraged him. Billy said his gift "did not make the Lord a bit more willing to save him, but it made him more willing to be saved;" and therefore he believed "the devil kept the thought out of the young man's mind as long as he could."

It is more important to speak of his deep piety, his abiding sense of the Divine favour, the secret of his great usefulness, the source of his constant and perpetual joy. The "much fruit," which is so pleasing to God, cannot come except the roots have struck deep into the soil. Religion is not shallow in its nature. "The water that I shall give you," said the Saviour, "shall be in you a *well of water* springing up into everlasting life." To be "sanctified wholly," to use an apostolic phrase, Billy very early in his religious history felt to be both his duty and privilege. "I remember being," he says, "at Hicks Mill Chapel one Sunday morning at class-meeting when a stranger led the class. The leader asked one of our members whether he could say that the Lord had cleansed him from all sin, and he could not. ' That,' I said in my mind, 'is sanctification: I will have that blessing by the help of the Lord;' and I went on my knees at once, and cried to the Lord to sanctify me wholly, body, spirit, soul. And the Lord said to me, 'Thou art clean through the word I have spoken unto thee.' And I said, 'Lord, I believe it.' When the leader came to me I told him, 'Four months ago I was a great sinner against God. Since that time I have been justified freely by His grace, and while I have been here this morning, the Lord has sanctified me wholly.' When I had done telling what the Lord had done for me, the leader said, 'If you can believe it, it is so.' Then I said, 'I can believe it.' When I had told him so, what joy filled my heart I cannot find words to tell. After meeting was over, I had to go over a railroad, and all around me seemed so full of glory that it dazzled my sight. I had a joy unspeakable, and full of glory." From one expression in this narrative some may dissent. It seems injudicious, to say the least, to tell a believer that he is sanctified if he believes he is, or to tell a penitent that he is saved if he only believes he is. There is a more excellent way. But henceforth Billy lived not to himself, but to Him who died for him and rose again. He set the Lord always before him. His path was like the shining light, his own favourite figure, that shineth more and more to the perfect day. *Justified, sanctified, sealed*, were successive steps in his Christian experience, more clear to him, perhaps, than to others. His faith did not become feeble, but waxed stronger and stronger; his love to his Saviour grew in intensity till it became the absorbing passion of his soul; and his hope brightened into heavenly radiance and splendour. The freshness, the gladsomeness, the delicacy and fragrance of the richest Christian experience seemed always to be his He soon reached, if we may borrow Bunyan's figure, the "Delectable Mountains," just in the way to the Celestial City, and which have "a pleasant prospect on every side." Happily, too, he carefully avoided traversing "the country of Conceit" which lieth near on the left hand, or sleeping in the place where "Little-Faith" lost "most of his spending money." Doubts and fears, "gloomy thoughts that rise," he knew but little about, "because he lived further up," thus escaping the thick fogs and mists which dull the hopes and becloud the prospects of ordinary Christians. He was, so one of his friends tells us, like a roe or young hart upon the mountains of Bether; on Zion he saw the glory of God between the cherubim; on Hermon the dew of God's blessing continually rested on him; on Carmel and Sharon he gathered flowers of every hue and of richest fragrance, while on Tabor all that was earthly and sorrowful in his experience was transfigured into the heavenly.

One of the most blessed results of his deep piety was his unfeigned humility. His estimate of himself in comparison with other Christians was that he was a coarse spar among beautiful specimens. He would say, "Most gentlemen have a grotto"—in Billy's sense a collection of mine specimens and other curiosities so arranged as to make things beautiful in themselves still more beautiful— in the centre of which "a coarse ould (old) spar would be generally placed. So the Lora nas His grotto—the Church, in which He places His own people as so many beautiful specimens, of different sizes, colours, and degrees of beauty, but all so arranged as to exhibit all the graces of the Spirit, and consequently constituting a very grand and beautiful sight:" Billy being only the "coarse ould spar among the rest to show their beauties to greater advantage," but with a heart bounding with gratitude and a tongue vibrating with praise because he was counted worthy of a place among the people of God.

At public meetings the idea would sometimes come out in a somewhat different fashion. The several speakers, and their brilliant, eloquent, and powerful speeches, reminded him of the precious stones with which the foundations of the heavenly Jerusalem were garnished, but the greatest wonder was that God, after having hewn these out of different quarries, and made them polished stones in His glorious temple, should pick up "an ould Cornish spar" to set off their great and manifold excellences with still greater effect. And then casting a look upward, a still greater wonder was it that Jehovah, from "His glorious high throne," should stoop to fetch up *such* an "ould" spar from His footstool to increase the splendour and magnificence of His palace; and then He would anticipate the time when he, a young Prince, a son of the King of kings, should, in company with the seraphs, traverse the golden streets, and make the heavenly arches ring with his loud praises. Before he had finished, the misers, laden with gold and sinking under its weight like a hippopotamus in a bed of mud, might be told that they could not be admitted except the keenest of angels were first appointed to watch them continually, for fear they should tear up the golden pavement to hug it to their bosoms in the vain hope of filling that mighty void which God alone can fill. His practical and sound advice to them would be, "Use all your earthly possessions to make 'lifting steps' to reach the highest place possible in the New Jerusalem, my happy home above."

Billy's idea above reminds us of a beautiful passage in the *Sermons* of the Rev. John Ker, but even by the side of his graceful eloquence, Billy's rude picture is not without its charms. Mr Ker says, "There is a different colour of beauty in different stones that are all of them precious. One man may be burnishing to the sparkle of the diamond, while another is deepening to the glow of the ruby. For this reason there are such different temperaments in Christian character, and varying circumstances in Christian life, that the foundation of the wall of the city may be garnished with all manner of precious stones.......It is very beautiful to see how the God, who has bound His world into a grand harmony by its very diversity, has arranged for this same end in His Church by giving the members their different faculties of work, —how the pure light that comes from the sun breaks into its separate hues when it touches the palace-house of Christ with its varied cornices and turrets, till every colour lies in tranquil beauty beside its fellow."

His humility was his safeguard all through life. An aged person remembers hearing him say on one occasion: "Soon after I was converted the devil said to me,

| SCRIPTURE TESTIMONY |
| :---: |
| *God using circumstances and timing to communicate* |
| ACTS II:II |

'Billy Bray, you'll be a great man *but I sunk into nothing, and in that way slipped through the devil's hand.*" Another result of Billy's deep piety was his *continual sense of dependence upon God.* The Lord's servants without the Lord's presence are weak like other men, like Samson when he lost his locks. Here is one "experience" of Billy's: "When I was in the St Neot Circuit, I was on the plan; and I remember that one Sunday I was planned at Redgate, and there was a chapel full of people, and the Lord gave me great power and liberty in speaking; but all at once the Lord took away His Spirit from me, so that I could not speak a word: and this might have been the best sermon that some of them ever heard. 'What!' you say, 'and looking like a fool, and not able to speak?' 'Yes,' for it was not long before I said, 'I am glad I am stopped, and that for *three* reasons. And the first is, To humble my soul, and make me feel more dependent on my Lord, to think more fully of Him, and less of myself. The next reason is, To convince you that you are ungodly, for you say we can speak what we have a mind to, without the Lord as well as with Him; but you cannot say so now, for you heard how I was speaking, but when the dear Lord took away His Spirit I could not say another word; without my Lord I could do nothing. And the third reason is, That some of you young men who are standing here, may be called to stand in the pulpit some day as I am; and the Lord may take His Spirit from you as He has from me, and then you might say, 'It is no good for me to try to preach or exhort, for I was stopped the last time I tried to preach, and I shall preach no more.' But now you can say, 'I saw the poor old Billy Bray stopped once like me, and he did not mind it, and told the people that he was glad his dear Lord had stopped him, and Billy Bray's dear Lord is my Lord, and I am glad He stopped me too, for if I can benefit the people, and glorify God, *that* is what I want.' I then spoke a great while, and told the people what the dear Lord gave me to say."

He kept the great object of life before him wherever he went, whatever he did. Thus he writes, "I was a ked to go to the re-opening of a chapel. We had large congregations. I spoke in the forenoon, and brother Coles in the afternoon and evening. He had the mighty power of God, and preached two very good sermons. The people were very kind in giving their money for repairing God's house. On the Monday they had a tea-meeting, and I had to speak at three o'clock. The tea was at five. I believe we should be better off if we were to fast and pray, and give the money without a tea; we should have more of the glory in our souls. In the evening we had a speaking meeting; one of our friends took the chair. He called on the superintendent to speak first; and after that he called on me. I told the people that the dear Lord had given them a pretty chapel to worship in; and now He wanted good furniture, for bad furniture looks disgraceful in a good house. I told them that good furniture for the house of the Lord was *sanctified souls*. We must be pardoned, sanctified, and sealed, and then we shall not only be fit for the Lord's house on earth, but we shall be *good furniture in heaven*."

He continued to be in "labours more abundant." His eye had a merry twinkle, his countenance an open and benevolent expression, his voice a cheerful and pleasant ring even unto the last. He took long journeys, held frequent services, had regular times for fasting and prayer —praise rather than prayer, especially at the last—and witnessed glorious victories even unto the end. His visits to the sick seemed more numerous even than before. The infirmities of age had come upon him, but his ruling passion had undergone no change, his spiritual ardour no abatement. One of his last entries, as late as February 10th, 1868, was, "In the morning after I had breakfast, bad as I was, I thought I would go to see some friends; and after calling on some of them, I went home. But I had hard work to get home, I was so ill; and my breath was short."

Only a little time before he had been at *Newlyn* and *Crantock*, labouring among the Wesleyans. There was a revival in progress in the latter place, and in a revival Billy was always at home.

"The dear Lord made the people very happy, and me happy with them." After the meeting in the chapel was closed one night, many of the people adjourned to a friend's

| SCRIPTURE TESTIMONY |
| :---: |
| *There is no sting in death for the believer* |
| I CORINTHIANS 15:54-57 |

house. There some were singing, some praising God, and others crying for mercy. Six souls were set at blessed liberty, and the meeting was continued till a very late hour. "We could do nothing but praise," Billy said, "for the Spirit was poured out in such a wonderful manner. I was as happy as I could be and live. It was one stream of glory." He was very weak in body then, but as the outward man decayed, the inward man was renewed day by day. "I think I shall be home to Fathers house soon," was his happy thought, his glorious hope. He returned home pale and exhausted. He left it but once afterwards, when he went to Liskeard to see his children. He got much worse, and appeared like a man in the last stage of consumption. On one occasion he sent for a medical man, and when he arrived he said: —"Now, doctor, I have sent for you because they tell me you are an honest man, and will tell the people the truth about their state." After the doctor had examined him, Billy said; "Well, doctor, how is it?" "You are going to die." Billy instantly shouted "Glory! glory be to God! I shall soon be in heaven." He then added in a low tone, and in his own peculiar way, "When I get up there, shall I give them your compliments, doctor, and tell them you will be coming too?" This, the doctor says, "made a wonderful impression upon him." It scarcely need be said that Billy retained all his old love for shouting; he even said if he had his time to go over again he would shout ten times as much, in his affliction he was visited by persons of all denominations, who liberally contributed to his support. On Friday, May 22nd, 1868, he came down stairs for the last time. To one of his old friends, a few hours before his death, who asked if he had any fear of death, or of being lost, he said, "What! me fear death! me lost! Why, my Saviour conquered death. If I was to go down to hell I would shout glory! glory!

to my blessed Jesus until I made the bottomless pit ring again, and the miserable old Satan would say, 'Billy, Billy, this is no place for thee: get thee back.' Then up to heaven I should go, shouting glory! glory! praise the Lord!" A little later he said, "Glory!" which was his last word, and in a little time his was the unspeakable joy to behold that glory which Jesus had with the Father before the world was. He was blessing and praising the Lord all the day, so that heaven was not to him very different to earth; the soul, according to Wesley—

> "The change shall scarcely know,
> Made perfect first in love."

Glory in his experience had begun below, he enjoyed wonderful fore-tastes of its fulness and fruition in heaven above. He took his departure to the skies on Monday, May 25th, 1868, having reached the age of seventy-four years within a few days.

On the Friday following a large number of his friends and neighbours assembled at his house, when the corpse was brought out into the yard, and two appropriate addresses delivered, one by Mr J. D. Balkwill, Billy's pastor, and the other by Mr Thomas Hicks, an old and much-attached friend. His remains were interred at Baldhu Church, where they await the joyous resurrection to eternal life.

Our task is all but completed, and if possible we should, in a few closing words, like to set forth the character of Billy Bray and the lessons of his life more clearly and impressively than it has been done in the preceding pages. But we fear to make the attempt, and we rejoice to think that it can hardly be needed. The most careless reader must, we imagine, have thought while reading the foregoing account, that if Billy had not been a Christian, he had been nothing; and that the mere *form* of religion, with which many are easily satisfied, must have utterly failed to comfort and support him in his trials and temptations. Billy Bray was so greatly honoured and blessed himself, and made so great a blessing to many, because his religion was a glorious reality, part and parcel of his daily life and experience. To him all the promises of Christianity were true, all its privileges to be enjoyed, all its duties to be performed, and all its hopes and blessings to be realised. He was simple, earnest, honest, devout. He belonged to the illustrious "Peerage of Poverty." And he, like The Wall's-End Miner, The Village Blacksmith, The Shepherd of Salisbury Plain, shall delight and instruct multitudes in days yet to come by the beautiful simplicity and goodness of his character. Many have gone as safely as he to the heaven above, who have not left behind them *a line of heavenly light, a trail of eternal glory*, as he has done, to be the guide of others, and to stimulate them to follow him as he followed Christ.

At the request of many of Billy's friends, we append, with his consent, Mr Johns' poetical tribute to the memory of Billy: —

A DIRGE for the Cornish Miner,

> For Billy Bray the brave;
> He was not born to honour,
> Such as the world would crave;
> But in the vale of labour
> His lot it was to tread,
> Till Jesus called him higher,
> Where rests his weary head.
> His fare was sometimes scanty,
>
> And earnest was the fight;
> But his dear Lord provided,
> And with him all was right.
> His dress was always homely—
> His dwelling somewhat poor
> But the presence of his Saviour
> Made up for that, and more:
> While in his face contentment
>
> Was beaming like the sun;
> And so did it continue,
> Till life and toil were done
> His soul possessed of patience

The cross he meekly bore.
In honour of his Master,
Who did the like before.
He had a cottage-closet,

In which he loved to dwell,
In secret heart-up-breathing,
A duty prized he well;
So God his Heavenly Father
Might, through him, ever be
Adored and highly honoured,
And he His glory see.

The Bible was his Guide-book,
In which he daily read
Of Jesus Christ who died,
But not of Christ the dead;
And drinking thus of water,
So living, full, and clear,
He every day had strength
To combat sin and fear.

In many a congregation
His voice was often heard,
Proclaiming free salvation,
Through Christ the living Word;
In manner, gentle, simple,
In spirit, kind and rare,
His life one holy living
Of humble, earnest prayer.

The aged and afflicted,
The mourner bending low,
Found in him a comforter,

Such as but few could know.
But now his work is ended,
His journey o'er and done;
With earth he too has finished,
With heaven just begun.

Nor doubt we for a moment,
He and the angels vie,
In the land of sweetest pleasure,
Where goodness cannot die.
Over the swelling river,
Where fields are always green;
With Billy Bray the famous,
How changed must be the scene!

High on the hills of Eden,
With angels on the wing;
Shouting his favourite saying,
"I AM THE SON OF A KING! "
Climbing the dew-clad mountain
Of God's eternal truth,
In all the vigour of manhood,
In all the beauty of youth

A basking in the fulness
Of that eternal day;
Where beauty ever brightens,
And pleasures ne'er decay:
Where glory, fairer, greater,
Than ever warrior won,
Shall gild his path for ever,
E'en brighter than the sun.

A dancing to the harpers.
On floors of solid gold;
Where the music's ever new,
And the song never old:
A dweller with the angels—
At home among the blest;
"Where the wicked cease from troubling,
And the weary are at rest."

So much for his religion,
Saving in all her powers;
Whate'er our rank or station,
God grant the like be ours!
Then in this higher life-land,
We meet again ere long;
Where tears shall all be wiped away,
And every note a songs

# SCRIPTURE TESTIMONY INDEX

**The believer is to be persistent in prayer** ................................... 18
*Luke 11:5-10*

For Billy, prayer was life and he lived every day conscious of his power-lessness without it. So he prayed, without ceasing and without doubting.

**Disciples were filled with joy and the Holy Spirit** ....................... 25
*Acts 13:52*

During an early morning walk together, Mr. Oliver shared thoughts about heaven, leading Billy to praise the Lord out of joy, with tears in his eyes. Billy's joyous enthusiasm led him to encourage others to join him in praising God, firmly believing that everyone should sing God's praise ardently, like a young prince.

**Death for the believer is to be with Christ** ................................. 26
*Philippians 1:21-23 · 1 Thessalonians 4:13*

Billy Bray, a devout Christian, exemplified the virtue of rejoicing, pray-ing, and giving thanks in all circumstances, even when faced with sorrow and trials. His unwavering faith and joy in God's love allowed him to find peace and comfort, leading him to praise and celebrate in times of both joy and sorrow. Billy's belief in the afterlife and his desire to share the glory of heaven with others fueled his unshakable optimism and constant praise of God's love and blessings.

**Whether we live or die, we are the Lord's** ................................... 28
*Romans 14:7-8*

Billy Bray, a joyful man of faith, lived a life of constant praise and exuberance for the Lord. His infectious spirit led him to encourage others to join in praising God and to always keep their spiritual "wheels" well-oiled and ready for service.

**God's work will not lack God's supply** ...................................... 34
*Philippians 4:19*

Billy Bray faced intense opposition to building a church that God had commanded him to build. When the church is complete, it became an important meeting place for believers. Some of those who had opposed him returned to ask for his forgiveness, and he forgave them.

**God answers prayer**................................................................ 36
*Luke 18:7 · John 15:7 · Acts 12:5 · James 5:15*

Billy Bray was tempted during the illness of his daughter. Rather than succumb to temptation, he prayed to God for divine healing. His daughter was healed immediately and her testimony made Billy bolder.

**Fervently and zealously serve the Lord** ...................................... 39
*Romans 12:11*

Poor Billy is directed by the Lord to build a chapel at Kerley Downs. Despite facing challenges and lack of support from others, with the help of his son and the Lord's strength, he worked tirelessly, even juggling work in the mine, to fulfill this task. Through dedication and faith, he managed to overcome obstacles and complete the chapel project.

**God using an inner voice to communicate** .............................. 42
*John 14:26 · Acts 10:19-20 · Acts 11:12*

Billy Bray shared his experiences of building a chapel in Gwennap, with the Lord's help. He recounts how he received donations for materials, including a memorable encounter with a reluctant giver in Helston. Ned also describes a successful fishing venture in St Ives, where the community's prayers for a good catch were answered, providing funds for the chapel.

**Ask Me anything in My name** .................................................. 45
*Matthew 18:19 · John 14:13-14 · John 16:23-24*

Billy Bray is excited to find an old cupboard to use as a pulpit for the little chapel at Kerley Downs, but is outbid at an auction and worries about returning the money. Fortunately, a man offers to sell it to Billy for the original price, and Billy interprets this as a sign that God intervened to help him acquire the pulpit.

**God gave signs and wonders through the apostles** ...................... 49
*Acts 5:12*

Dorothea Trudel turns to prayer for five of her employees who have become unwell after all other options have failed. They were all able to recover. As word of this spread, a large number of people approached her.

For seven years, Florence Hoskin relied on crutches to walk. She went to a session one day and was entirely healed, never having to use crutches again. Many others came to see "what a miracle the loving Lord had wrought" after hearing of her healing.

A man named 'grandfather' who was very lame was healed by a prayer from Billy Bray when they were headed to Kestle Mill for a teetotal meeting. 'Grandfather' shared his story of transformation from being a drunkard to a teetotaler after his healing experience during the meeting, leading to 20 people signing the pledge.

Billy Bray was known for his generosity and devotion to both God and others. He gladly shared his belongings with those in need, always putting his faith into action by seeking help for the poor and praying in rich and poor homes alike.

Billy visited devoted Christians like Peggy Mitchell who could read her "title clear to mansions in the skies," finding this duty rewarding and important as he shared messages of mercy and comfort with the sick. Young individuals from privileged backgrounds often joined him on his visits, all united as brothers and sisters in Christ, experiencing blessings and becoming blessings themselves as they spread love and cheer.

Billy was moved by his deep faith and asked the Lord for guidance on fasting. Despite concerns from others, he received a divine message confirming his practice of fasting. Billy felt spiritually and physically strengthened by his devotion to God, believing that following the Lord's will renewed him like an eagle.

Billy, a man of strong Christian values and integrity, upheld a strict moral code and refused to participate in dishonest practices, even at the risk of facing opposition. He believed that one cannot truly enjoy religion while engaging in deceit or fraud, and he remained steadfast in his commitment to maintain a clear conscience in all situations, regardless of the status of the offenders.

Billy Bray overcame his fear of encountering the spirits of the deceased at the mine. As he approached a shaft, thoughts of encountering the devil himself on a bridge provoked him to boldly proclaim his faith and trust in God, dispelling his fears and leading him to dance and sing praises in victory to the Lord in the end.

Billy Bray faced financial trials but remained faithful, trusting that the Lord would provide for him and his family even in times of scarcity. Despite criticism from his wife about his charitable giving, Billy remained steadfast in his belief that the Lord would always provide for them.

Billy borrowed ten shillings from the captain but instead gave it away to two families in need. Despite giving away the money, he expressed faith that the Lord would not leave him in debt, and his shoes were later replaced by a friend with new ones and other essential items, showing how his faith was rewarded.

A missionary preacher, inspired by the love of Christ, endured poverty and hardship to spread the Gospel. Despite facing temptation and challenges, his resolve remained strong, and he was eventually aided by kind Quaker friends who provided him with clothes and money. This man's dedication resulted in him becoming a great blessing in the community where he preached.

Billy Bray was a slave to the twin vice of drinking and smoking. But he became a free man when he yielded to the prompting to quit by the "small still voice within" him.

Billy encountered a man struggling with his faith after swearing in a moment of anger, feeling judged and disconnected. Prompted by a divine message, Billy intervened, offering support and encouragement to help the man regain his faith and find peace, while the man's wife, who continued to be cruel and harsh, faced her own consequences later on.

Billy Bray, a joyful Christian man, showed compassion and helped an old gentleman find peace and faith in God during his last days. Despite initial animosity, Billy's kindness and faith brought comfort and transformation to the old man, who found eternal brightness and joy upon his passing.

Billy Bray, a deeply pious man, credited his humility as protecting him throughout life. In one instance, sharing his experience in a sermon, he spoke about the importance of being reliant on God and how losing the Lord's presence humbled him and made him more aware of his dependence on the divine in his preaching.

Billy experienced great joy during a revival in Crantock. Despite his physical weakness, he remained hopeful and eager to join his Father in heaven, welcoming death with shouts of glory. His last words were filled with praise and anticipation of the glory he would experience in the afterlife.

# MORE BIOGRAPHIES
## FROM
# WALKING TOGETHER PRESS

### RECOLLECTIONS OF AN EVANGELIST
#### *by Robert Gribble*

Robert Gribble was a simple, uneducated man, who worked with simple, uneducated farmers and laborers in the villages of the bucolic Devonshire countryside. Perhaps surprising to a modern reader, rural Britain in the first part of the nineteenth century was unreached with the Gospel. Robert Gribble worked with people in a post-Christian time much like our own.

### INCIDENTS IN THE LIFE OF
### EDWARD WRIGHT
#### *by Edward Leach*

Born in 1836, Edward "Ned" Wright led a life of vice and crime. His days were filled with drinking, smoking, wife-beating, and stealing-even stealing from the dead. It seemed impossible that he could ever reform. But then one night something happened. Out of curiosity, Ned and his wife went into a fancy theater for an "all seats free" program. There they were unexpectedly and powerfully affected by a Gospel presentation during which Ned was carried away into a waking vision of "the most awful tribunal I ever witnessed..."

## GEORGE MÜLLER OF BRISTOL
### *by Arthur T. Pierson*

Imagine a man walking into a poor rural village containing thousands of people and then promising to take care of their every need; food, clothing, housing, education. And then imagine that he proposed to do this without telling anyone other than God that these needs even existed. This man was George Müller, and that village was the more than ten thousand orphans for whom he cared, over sixty years of his life.

## DR. BAEDEKER
## AND HIS APOSTOLIC WORK
## IN RUSSIA
### *by R. S. Latimer*

Through aristocratic connections, God granted Dr. Baedeker unprecedented access to the horrible prisons of Czarist Russia. He chose to use his material success and position of the first forty years of his life to serve the poor and the lowliest for the next forty years of his life.

### MARY SLESSOR OF CALABAR
*by W. P. Livingstone*

Mary Slessor was a missionary to Nigeria. She identified with and endeared herself to the people. She defended the weak and adopted twins that were destined for destruction, ultimately bringing an end to twin infanticide. Today, more than one hundred years later, Mary Slessor is still celebrated in Calabar, Nigeria. Her statue stands in the center of the city, a memorial to a woman whose life was a blessing to this people. She is depicted holding infant twins.

### SADHU SUNDAR SINGH
*by C. F. Andrews*

In a time of profound personal crisis, in which his lifetime of intense spiritual devotion still offered no peace, Sundar Singh was defeated and determined to kill himself if he could not find the True God. Half an hour before the appointed time with the deadly train track, he had a vision of Jesus Christ, the one who saves. This encounter forever changed Sundar Singh and set him on the path of being a Christian Sadhu, or holy man, who-with "neither purse, nor scrip"-walked barefoot from village to village and over mountain passes to Tibet, preaching the Good News of Jesus Christ.

## HUDSON TAYLOR
## THE MAN WHO BELIEVED GOD
### *by Marshall Broomhall*

Hudson Taylor was as a missionary to China and founder of the China Inland Mission. He lived by faith, trusting only God for all temporal supplies for himself, his family, and more than eight hundred missionaries that joined him in decades of Gospel labor. Through all this, Hudson Taylor was first and foremost a child of God, constantly growing in his faith. One of Taylor's greatest gifts to posterity is the transparency with which he wrote about life challenges and his own faith journey.

## GOFORTH OF CHINA
## BY HIS WIFE
### *by Rosalind Goforth*

Almost from the moment of his conversion at eighteen years of age, Jonathan Goforth was an evangelist. In addition to tireless itinerant preaching, constant evangelism in slums, and even brothels; one summer during his years at Knox College, he visited nine hundred sixty Toronto families. It was said of Jonathan Goforth that, "When he found his own soul needed Jesus Christ, it became a passion with him to take Jesus Christ to every soul." This passion-which led him to devote his life to the cause of spreading the Gospel in China-resonated with a twenty-year-old artist who, after surreptitiously examining Goforth's heavily annotated Bible, said to herself, "This is the man I would like to marry!"

## MIMOSA
### *by Amy Carmichael*

This little book tells a highly unusual story. Taking place, as it does, in an early 1900's rural Hindu village, and with Amy Carmichael's artful telling, it seems like some kind of tragic fairytale. In fact, at one point the author asks the reader, "Does it read like a story made up, or at least touched up a little?" But it is not a story made up. Carmichael says, "Of all the stories we have touched since we came to India, hardly one has humbled us so much, as we thought of our faithless fears for the little Mimosa. But hardly one has lifted us so high in adoration, and in wonder, and in awe."

How could a little girl who only spent one afternoon in the company of real Christians, gain enough light, or glean enough crumbs from under the Master's table, to sustain a profound and effectual faith through her many years of suffering? How could she learn about her loving Father in heaven, whom she asked to gather her and her children under the safety of His wings-like a hen gathers her chicks-without ever hearing or reading (she was illiterate) Luke 13:34? How did she find the conviction and the strength to resist the sometimes violent pressure to participate in the all-pervasive idol-worship of her community? How indeed, except that her loving Father taught her and sustained her. This story poses challenging questions about the very nature of living by faith.

# TESTIMONIES OF FAITH
## FROM
# WALKING TOGETHER PRESS

**OUR FAITHFUL GOD**
**ANSWERS TO PRAYER**
*by James H. Smith*

*Our Faithful God: Answers to Prayer* is an inspiring collection of testimonies that demonstrate the power of prayer in the lives of those who follow Jesus, showing the diverse ways in which God answers prayer, provides guidance, grace, and blessings both in everyday situations and in times of great need. Whether you are seeking guidance, comfort, or simply a reminder of God's love and presence in your life, you'll find this book a timeless and invaluable companion.

**HOW I KNOW GOD ANSWERS PRAYER**
*by Rosalind Goforth*

*How I Know God Answers Prayer* is a collection of Jonathan and Rosalind Goforth's personal testimonies to answered prayer during their lives as missionaries to China, including barely surviving the 1900 Boxer Rebellion.

## MIRACLE LIVES OF CHINA
### *by Jonathan & Rosalind Goforth*

*Miracle Lives of China* paints a vivid portrait of this transformative power by telling the amazing and captivating stories of individuals, from addicted gamblers and learned scholars, to children, soldiers, and the aged, whose lives were radically altered by the redeeming power of the Gospel. This precious collection is a testament to God's enduring love. It reminds us that, regardless of our background or the depth of our sin, no life is beyond the reach of His saving grace.

## CHINESE DIAMONDS FOR THE KING OF KINGS
### *by Rosalind Goforth*

These sketches of real people, and their stories of redemption and refinement, reveal human gem stones set apart for the King of Kings. God is able to do the miraculous, bringing the lowly opium addict up from the dirt, or the proud scholar down from his pedestal, transforming them both into brothers and sisters-peers-in the Kingdom family. Story after story in this small book testify to the reality of God and the truth of His word.

## BY MY SPIRIT
### *by Jonathan Goforth*

Jonathan and Rosalind Goforth were Presbyterian missionaries in China from 1888 to 1935. In the early 1900's, Mr. Goforth became a student of revivals, both contemporary and historical, and for the rest of his missionary career he worked as an evangelist and revivalist. This book is the astonishing record of the Holy Spirit's work in meeting after meeting, and contains dozens of stories testifying to the reality of God and the truth of His Word.

## ANSWERED OR UNANSWERED
### *by Louisa Vaughan*

This is the challenge posed to the reader by the eighteen stories of prayer in this little book. Louisa Vaughan was a Presbyterian missionary in China who lived in the present reality of God, and wrote this beautiful and engaging collection of stories testifying to that reality. Two subjects of faith recur in almost every story; that the believer can ask anything in the name of Jesus based on His promise in John 14:13-14, and that via prayer and repentance, genuine revival comes through a visitation of the Holy Spirit.

## THE NEW ACTS OF THE APOSTLES
### *by Arthur T. Pierson*

A sweeping biographical survey of Protestant missions in the eighteenth and nineteenth centuries, *The New Acts of the Apostles* demonstrates the thesis that God's work of bringing the Gospel of Jesus Christ to the ends of the earth has continued uninterrupted from the New Testament Book of Acts up to the present day. We are, in effect, living out additional chapters of the story that began in Acts. Filled with exciting and inspirational stories, Pierson's book introduces the reader to dozens of missionary heroes and devoted followers of Jesus. He shows how they relied upon God to provide and to move in power for the increase of His Kingdom, in ways that parallel the stories of the first Apostles.

### THE GOOD BOOKS DEVOTIONAL
### VOLUME I
*by D. Thaine Norris*

Unsure of which of these life-changing Christian Classics to read first? Start with our devotional!

What kind of a title is the "Good Books" devotional? If this book were written 150 years ago we might have titled this little volume, "The Devotional that Seeks to Introduce the Reader to an Indispensable Collection of Must-Read Titles from the Public Domain, Volume I," because that is what it seeks to do.

Written as a companion to the Scripture Testimony Collection, this book aims to explain why each title in the collection is worth reading. Everyone faces the problem of trying to convince a friend to read a good book they have never heard of before. This daily devotional is intended both to draw out powerful spiritual lessons from real-life stories, and as a way for us at Walking Together Press to say, "What? You have never heard of this book? Here, let me read you this short excerpt…"

The following titles are covered in this devotional:

*Answered or Unanswered?*

*By My Spirit*

*Chinese Diamonds for the King of Kings*

*Dr. Baedeker and His Apostolic Work in Russia*

*George Müller of Bristol*

*Goforth of China*

*How I know God Answers Prayer*

*Hudson Taylor: The Man who believed God*

*Mimosa*

*Recollections of an Evangelist*

*Sadhu Sundar Singh*

**_Walking Together Press_** is a non-profit publishing company devoted to supporting grassroots libraries in Africa through global book sales and through providing free library editions.

To read our story, to see our catalog, and to learn more about how you can help us in our mission, visit our website at:

walkingtogether.press

www.ingramcontent.com/pod-product-compliance
Lightning Source LLC
Chambersburg PA
CBHW020405130626
46549CB00006B/2442